German [illegible]c Policy and the Euro 1999-2010

Richard Conquest

ISBN: 978-0-9564614-2-1

Published in February 2011 by
The Bruges Group, 227 Linen Hall, 162-168 Regent Street, London W1B 5TB
www.brugesgroup.com

Bruges Group publications are not intended to represent a corporate view of European and international developments. Contributions are chosen on the basis of their intellectual rigour and their ability to open up new avenues for debate.

About the Author

Richard Conquest is an economist, hedge fund consultant and author whose research focuses on the many aspects of contemporary economic history and events, market developments and crises. Richard has also authored a number of publications on Eastern Europe and Russia which have been used by the Foreign Office for graduate training.

He has also authored a number of highly prescient publications, including;

- *How Dangerous is the US Housing Market?* Published in September 2006, where he made the first City warning of the financial and economic dangers inherent in that market.
- He also made an early warning to the bond markets that British fiscal policy was dangerously incoherent and economically misaligned in his November 2006 publication titled *Gordon Brown: An Entirely Underserved Reputation.*
- In March 2009 he also authored the Bruges Group publication I*s the Euro Sustainable?* This was an analysis of the growing imbalances in the Eurozone and warning of the trouble to come.

He has had a career working in the financial sectors of many different countries. Richard was Chief Economist at the Japanese financial institution, Daiwa Securities. At Daiwa he also ran the Daiwa Securities Research Institute, here he was involved in a very wide range of research activities and became particularly involved in the economics of change in Eastern Europe and the Former Soviet Union. Richard has also conducted research at the London School of Economics.

Richard has also worked for ABN AMRO in Amsterdam and in the City of London for Skandinaviska Enskilda Banken (SEB) and at the UK Treasury.

Table of Contents

EXECUTIVE SUMMARY

Introduction

The aim of this paper is to assess to what extent Germany - whether by accident or design - has been a beneficiary of the Euro era, and what negative impact, if any, there has been on the Eurozone's smaller economies.

Analysis shows that trade imbalances within the Eurozone centre upon Germany, the most important economy, and by far the largest exporting nation. Germany has substantial trade and current account surpluses with the other Eurozone members. In the last three recorded years for example, it was €114.3 billion in 2007, and €104.5 billion and €79.7 billion in the recession years of 2008 and 2009 respectively.

This situation is greatly exacerbated by the ECB's exchange rate policy which (wittingly or not) favours German interests. This is because, at the outset, the German people gave up their beloved D-Mark under an implicit agreement that EMU would never lead to inflation in their country. For this reason the European Central Bank tightens monetary policy whenever the German economy is in danger of over-heating, regardless of the needs of the Mediterranean economies.

The ECB's Exchange Rate Policy

The ECB's exchange rate policy centres upon the devaluation, not of the Nominal Exchange Rate which is 'irrevocably fixed' but rather by the devaluation of the Real Effective Exchange Rate. Within the Euro it is not possible to 'fix' the Real Effective Exchange Rate.

The ECB not only imposes an inappropriate interest rate policy upon the Eurozone, it also imposes an exchange rate which in essence suits the German economy but many Eurozone economies are finding it increasingly difficult to live with.

In the post-war period, Germany has been an export led economy; domestic demand contributes little to its economic dynamism. Thus, Germany's highly competitive industrial sector generates huge exportable surpluses while weak domestic demand means that import demand is lacklustre. The result is very large trade and current account surpluses.

This is more the case because during the era of the Euro, Germany has gained in competitiveness, while other countries, e.g. Italy, have lost competitiveness and, of course, no longer have the option of devaluation.

Germany's exchange rate policy is centred upon the labour market which is highly skilled and which demonstrates the most extraordinary self-discipline in the cause of preserving both jobs and competitiveness.

Thus, critical factors determining competitiveness: the level of wages, wage increases, working practices and the constant search for higher productivity have produced a situation in which Germany's Unit Labour Costs are extremely competitive. Other Eurozone countries, particularly in the Mediterranean-Rim, have proved unable to replicate this model.

The result is that the competitive advantage gained by Germany since the functioning Euro was introduced in 2002, is all but impossible to reverse or modify – a state of affairs in which German political leaders during this period, including current Chancellor Angela Merkel, have to date displayed no interest or concern.

This has proved damaging because it is very unlikely that countries such as Greece, Italy, Spain and Portugal will be able to restore their competitiveness to anything like the extent necessary to even start to narrow these imbalances.

The result is that the full weight of policy has been centred upon fiscal austerity and the suppression of domestic demand within the deficit countries, which means that the Mediterranean-Rim countries are having to borrow. This only increases their external debt, in effect to finance Germany's trade and current account surpluses – a state of affairs which is clearly unsustainable.

Germany's Pattern of Trade and Payments

Germany's pattern of trade and payments displays two undesirable characteristics: firstly, that Germany's export trade is too concentrated upon Europe. Secondly, and as a consequence of this, Germany's trade surplus is largely generated within Europe.

The combination of exchange rate developments and domestic economic conditions, especially weak domestic demand in Germany itself, makes this outcome inevitable. In this the Euro is not a self-correcting mechanism – on the contrary it serves to confirm such imbalances.

This situation is also a product of flawed policy decisions. With hindsight, it was mistake to allow countries with very large current account deficits to join the Euro.

It was known at the time that several countries that joined the Euro in 2002 – notably Greece and Portugal - already had evident balance of payments problems, typically, trade deficits. In 2007 on the eve of the credit crunch, no less than seven countries had current account deficits of more than 5% of GDP.

With hindsight, to expose these countries to competition with their strongest competitors and with fixed exchange rates appears to have been the height of economic folly. But, such was the enthusiasm for the Euro project that no one realised the danger.

Political Considerations

At the time of the negotiations for the establishing of the Euro, it was not economic considerations which were pre-occupying the Heads of Government and Finance Ministers, but political ones. E.g.

Wim Duisenburg, President of the European Central Bank, said on 1st January 1999 that *"From now on, monetary policy, usually an essential part of national sovereignty, will be decided by a truly European institution."*

Furthermore, Carlo Azeglio Ciampi, the Italian Minister of the Exchequer, Budget and Economy Programming also said at the time of the Euros launch that; *"It is a decisive step towards ever closer political and institutional union in Europe. Above all, it is political."* Yet his country is amongst those that are now paying a high financial price for this folly.

The former Italian Prime Minister Lamberto Dini also said that *"The decision to create a single currency in Europe was an eminently political decision. It was supposed to bring about greater European integration not only at an economic level, but at a political one."*

It is not surprising that in their excitement they failed to properly consider the economic implications of entering into a monetary union with Germany. Dominique Strauss-Kahn, the French Finance Minister when the Euro was launched even said that *"The Euro is a conquest of sovereignty. It gives us a margin of manoeuvre. It's a tool to help us master globalisation and help us resist irrational shifts in the market."*

Yet Romano Prodi, the Former President of the European Commission, still said on 20th May 2010 that *"When the euro was born everyone knew that sooner or later a crisis would occur... "We are therefore at a crossroads. The only alternative to greater co-ordination of economic policies is dissolution of the euro."*

It is clear, as many Italian politicians have recognised over the years that some countries would be better off out of the Euro and there are clear economic reasons for agreeing that this would be the best long run solution.

Political leaders are beginning to realise that the problem stems from the deliberate conduct of German economic policy. This is causing divisions even between Germany and their main ally France. These political tensions will only grow. Political figures such as Christine Lagarde, the French Minister of Economic Affairs, Finances and Industry, has already complained about German policy causing increasingly serious imbalances within the Eurozone. And in an interview with the *Financial Times* called on Germany to alleviate the problem it was causing.

> "[Could] *those with surpluses* [Germany] *do a little something? It takes two to tango. It cannot just be about enforcing deficit principles.*
>
> *"Clearly Germany has done an awfully good job in the last 10 years or so, improving competitiveness, putting very high pressure on its labour costs. When you look at unit labour costs to Germany, they have done a tremendous job in that respect. I'm not sure it is a sustainable model for the long term and for the whole of the group. Clearly we need better convergence."*

There is no easy solution to this but the Euro's disintegration would be economically beneficial in the long term. The example of the UK, which left the EU's Exchange Rate Mechanism on 16th September 1992, illustrates that there is life after the Euro.

The response from the elite so far is denial. Jean Claude Juncker is perhaps the leading advocate of the idea of issuing bonds commonly within the Eurozone. In this he is supported by EU Commission President Herman Van Rompuy and unsurprisingly opposed by Chancellor Angela Merkel, as it will simply raise borrowing costs for Germany and reduce them for its (as it sees it) financially profligate trading partners.

For the other Eurozone leaders, is it possible that they still have not understood the effect of the huge disparity between their own economies and that of Germany, still less what do about it.

Conversely, it would appear that a growing number of Germany's elite are only too aware:

Leading German industrialist, Frank Asbeck, says of the Eurozone crisis:

> *"From a German standpoint we don't see any crisis ....Germany is the industrial heart of Europe and as long as the Euro is weak, I think for Germany, it is a good situation."* (*Crossing Continents,* Friday, 14th January 2011, BBC Radio 4)

In fact, so great has been the advantage accorded to Germany by its membership of the Euro, that leading German economist Klaus Schweinsberg says:

> *"The big winner of the Eurozone is German industry...the view of the German industrialists is that ... it makes us relatively more competitive within the Eurozone"*

He further states that the German economy:

> *"has boomed to such an extent that Germany can afford to pay off the debts of Greece, Ireland and Portugal and should do so to preserve its export markets in those countries."* (*Crossing Continents,* Friday, 14th January 2011, BBC Radio 4)

Whatever the solution however, what cannot be disputed is that the German economy is the winner of the Euro era.

Why the Euro cannot survive with Germany at its centre

The protracted financial and economic crisis that has afflicted Greece and Ireland and which is inevitably threatening several other sovereign debtors with a 'contagion effect' - has variously been described as 'the first great test of the euro' and 'the most serious test' of that supposed currency. What is certain is that if this is the first or even second crisis it will not have been the last. This is because one of the underlying causes of the crisis has been concealed for reasons of political expediency and ideological fervour. The policy responses to the crisis, which is both fiscal and monetary in nature, centre only upon the correction of past fiscal and financial profligacy. The monetary dimension of the crisis is simply unmentionable in polite Brussels and Frankfurt society and for very good reasons.

The political elite of the European Union, wedded as it is to an irrational monetary ideology that owes nothing to economic theory or history but much to political Millenarianism, could never admit or allow that monetary causes have added greatly to the malaise of the Eurozone. It is clear that the economic problems of Greece and other Mediterranean-Rim economies, have been greatly exacerbated by a grotesque distortion of monetary policy which takes the form of the Euro itself.

The greatest danger is that to recognise this monetary cause, partial as it inevitably is, would immediately indicate that the Euro is seriously flawed and is unworkable in anything but the short term perspective without serious economic and financial distortions which have already become painfully evident. Because these problems will not be properly addressed then existing financial distortions will continue threatening financial paralysis and the collapse, both politically and economically, of the entire 'Euro' edifice. The bond markets are already shouting this from the rooftops – indeed they have been doing this for many months.

This can be clearly seen in the following chart which shows the yields or financial return on ten year government bonds. With the approach to the formation of the Eurozone it was argued that membership would reduce the risk on government debt and so bond yields converged. Of course it was always illusory and with the onset of the credit crunch the market quickly realised that some economies, notably those of the Mediterranean Rim, Greece, Italy, Spain and Portugal were much more vulnerable to economic and financial shocks than the staid economies of northern Europe.

Bond yields have thus widened so that risk premiums in the government debt market more accurately reflect the order of financial risk within Europe. The myth that the Eurozone reduces financial risk has been well and truly exposed. As will be argued below, this does not prevent such figures as 'President' Herman Van Rompuy and Jean Claude Juncker from attempting once more to conceal the nature of these risks by creating an EU bond to displace those issued by national governments. This is quite disgraceful and will fool nobody.

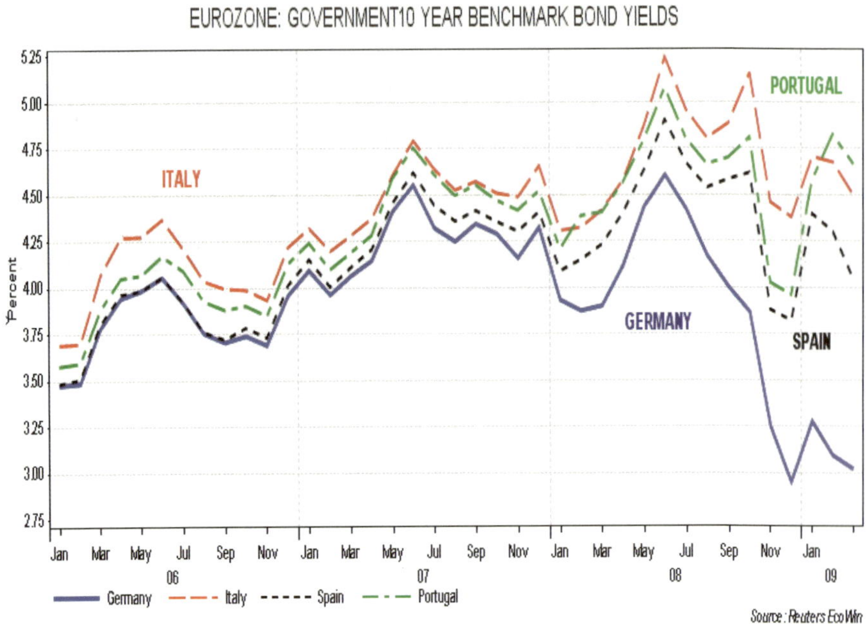

10 Year Government Bond Yields – Greece, Spain, France, Germany

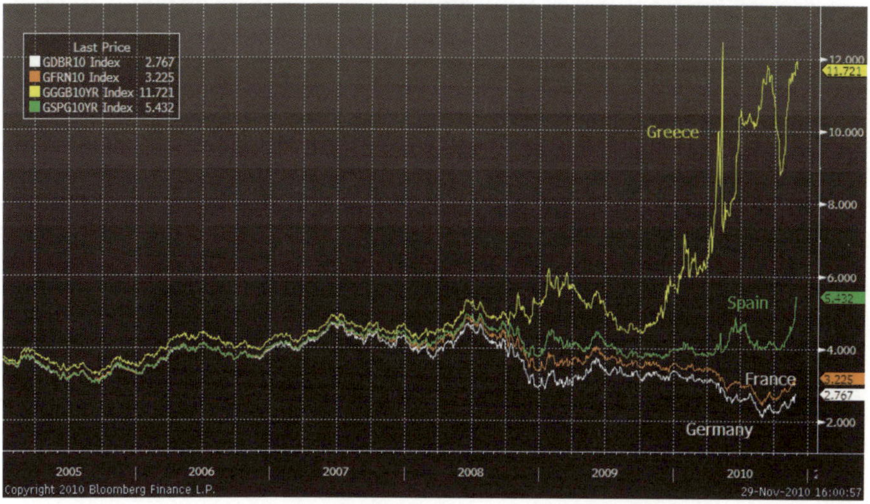

This chart maps the development of the yields of ten year government bonds. As can be seen there was a very artificial convergence of bond yields in the run up to the introduction of the Euro. The very idea that Greek government debt was on a par with that of Germany was always absurd and the steep divergence of yields simply reflects the market appraisal of the relatively high level of risk of some government debt – especially when compared to Germany. It means that the markets are demanding a higher risk premium from some sovereign borrowers.

The realities of the situation cannot be freely admitted by the political elite because to attribute any of the blame for Europe's malaise to the Euro would at once confirm the worst suspicions of the financial markets and precipitate a market-driven crisis that would quickly pass beyond the control of any government. Or, indeed pseudo-government such as the Brussels establishment. As time goes on this situation will only become more acute and crises more violent and economically destructive. So, for the time being at least, denial by the elite is the most expedient stance – stating and insisting upon that which they know to be untrue.

Most worrying of all, perhaps, is the fact that the President of the European Central Bank, Jean Claude Trichet, speaks in very much the same terms as the political class. He does not pursue an impartial, objective assessment of economic conditions which would allow the formulation of an appropriate monetary policy response. This is after all the proper function of a central bank governor. But no, rather, he serves an overtly political purpose. It is not for him to say, for example, which countries should remain in the Eurozone and which should leave. He flatly denies the possibility of the latter option, a manifestly absurd and very political position. History dictates that the politicisation of money always ends in disaster and Trichet is working actively to remind us of the validity of this observation.

It was always clear that the 'one fits all' notion of monetary policy would not work in the long run, especially when applied to such a disparate group of economies, of different structures, stages of economic evolution and at different stages of the business cycle; equally importantly, all functioning within the confines of their own unique political cultures. The last point is actually of enormous importance as the political tensions between Germany, Greece and Ireland have demonstrated. Furthermore, the monetary rivalry between Germany and France, so admirably described by David Marsh, in his book *The Euro – The Politics of the New Global Currency*, again shows how vitally important differences in political culture are. Thus, it is equally difficult to envisage how one government can function in such a disparate group of political cultures.

The Single Currency has inevitably resulted in a monetary policy, in terms of interest rates, that would be too restrictive for some slow growing economies and overly accommodative for others enjoying more dynamic growth rates. This could only ever result in excessive monetary stimulus in some economies and deflationary monetary impulses in others. Thus, the idea that the Euro would bring about economic 'convergence' was always economically nonsensical. In actual fact the opposite is the more likely result, creating economic divergences which would not necessarily have been the case had each government retained the ability to implement a monetary policy that reflected the unique conditions of each individual economy.

A retrospective view of growth differentials in the Eurozone illustrates this point very well. The conspicuous anomalies here are Ireland and Spain which both grew much more rapidly than the Eurozone average even before the introduction of Euro notes and coins in 2002. Thus, growth was stimulated by the laxity of monetary policy to the point that both became bubble economies. Ireland in particular is now paying a very high price for these years of Euro-folly.

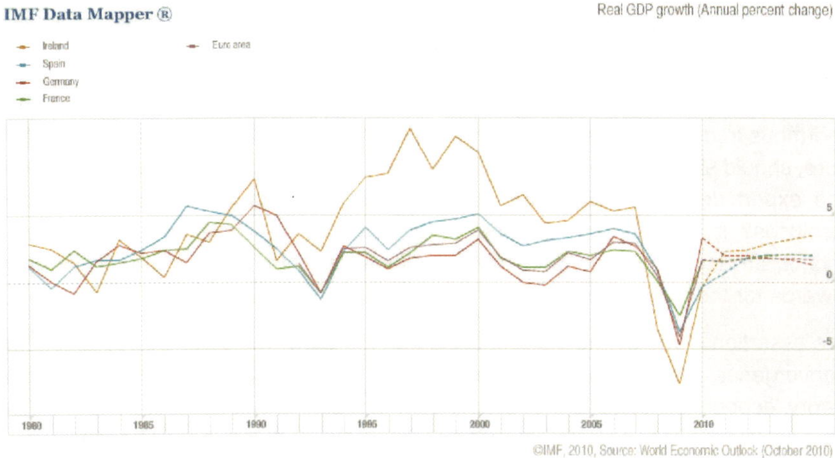

And there were of course, even weaker prospective Euro 'candidates' who followed the orthodoxy of ECB policy and none have paid a greater price than the Baltic States. Their political leaderships were seduced into thinking that EU and Euro membership were the final objectives of politico-economic policy. They were seduced into the bubble delusion of low EU interest rates when what they really required was far stricter monetary discipline. Incredibly, Estonia actually adopted the Euro in the New Year.

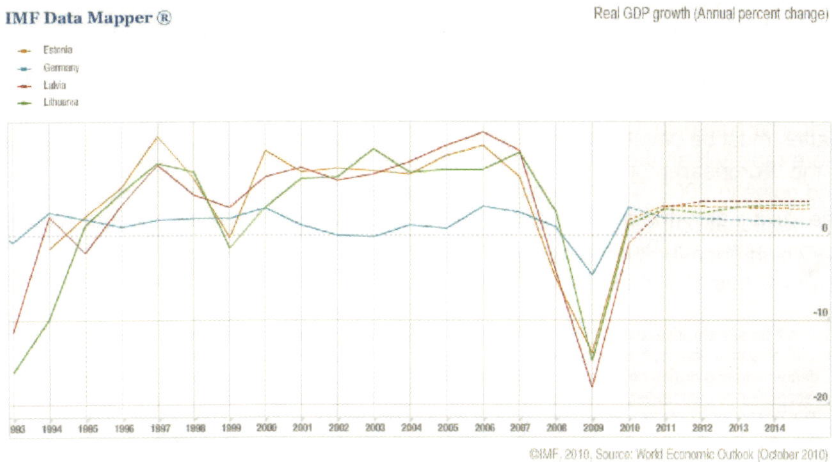

The artificiality of monetary policy in the Baltic States is indicated by the extraordinary extent of the collapse of economic activity – it has been like a re-run of the collapse of communism twenty years ago.

How could it ever have been *seriously* argued that the fast-growing Spain, with its enormous trade and current account deficits, apparent well before the coming of the Euro, should share a common interest and exchange rate policy with a slow-growing and export dependent Germany, luxuriating in huge trade and current account surpluses? It was always a recipe for disaster but the political class, including Trichet, are in their comfortable state of denial and of course, in receipt of lavish rewards for their incompetence.[1]

The assertion made by the political class that the Euro would bring about economic 'convergence' always stood in contradiction of the most basic tenets of economic theory, economic history and of simple common sense. After a decade of the Euro the price for the ideological perversion of Europe's monetary policy has to be paid. But this perversion will not end, the ruling elite will try every way possible to preserve this monetary Frankenstein of their making and at whatever cost to the taxpayer as the Irish and Germans are now finding out to their intense discomfiture.

This has so often been the case on previous occasions when the political manipulation of money has not worked: the politicians insist upon the rigid maintenance of such policies until the markets finally dictate crisis and devaluation. In the meantime the cost in terms of lost growth potential, unemployment, higher taxation and declining living standards, falls upon the blameless citizenry of 'Euroland'. This is precisely what the Greek and Irish electorates have been protesting about and they will not protest alone. Prime Minister John Major's futile 'defence' of sterling in 1992 is a perfect but by no means unique example of politicians defending the indefensible.

This is exactly the present situation. The failure of the Euro is not recognised for one second and so untold billions of taxpayers Euros, and pounds Sterling for that matter, must be devoted to maintaining the lie, covering up the all too obvious failure of the 'European project'.

The ruling elite themselves will never, of course, be called to account for their actions as they continue to enjoy the enormous privileges that the hapless European taxpayer bestows upon them. In this the elite is very similar to 'The New Class' as

1 Can it be any surprise to learn that Trichet is the latest recipient of the 'Vision for Europe' award? Previous laureates have included Jacques Santer, Jean-Claude Juncker, Jean-Luc Dehaene and Helmut Kohl, a depressing and dreary collection of functionaries in the 'leadership' of Europe. This award is granted 'in recognition of outstanding achievements in taking Europe into the future'; self-evidently an exercise in fatuity. The first recipient of this self-congratulatory award was Jacques Santer, former EU President, forced from his extravagant sinecure by Paul Van Buitenen's devastating accusations of corruption and fraud.

Milovan Djilas once described the emergence of a privileged, incompetent and corrupt ruling elite in Eastern Europe during the 1950s. It is extraordinary that while the Greek populace vents its frustration upon the political class, that class is more than ever content to see the further, the seemingly inexorable, advance of socialist corporatism in Brussels.

Of course, this advance should be challenged by parties of the centre-right but the Conservative Party in this country simply avoids the issue. It has ceased to be Conservative and has embraced the notions of socialist corporatism and that is why it could not defeat a derelict labour administration which had enjoyed thirteen years of power. Even more incredibly, David Cameron could not defeat an administration lead by the economically incompetent Gordon Brown. There are alternatives as Margaret Thatcher tried very bravely to set out in her famous Bruges speech in 1988 and again at Aspen Colorado in August 1990. Unfortunately, her words were drowned out by the din of approaching war in Iraq.

In conclusion it is now painfully evident that the adoption of the Euro by seventeen very disparate economies would not and could never produce the economic convergence and stability that the political elite so insistently proposed. On the contrary it could only ever produce economic *divergence* that would be destabilising and destructive. The problem then is that the elite have invested such immense amounts of political capital in this fatally flawed experiment that they cannot now admit to the enormity of their mistake. Thus, as with other failed fixed exchange rate regimes, of which there have been many, the elite will ignore all the lessons of economic theory and history – of which most of them are lamentably ignorant – and will attempt to prop up the Euro, no matter what the financial, economic and social cost, until the markets and the electorates of these ensnared countries finally rebel.

Exchange Rates and Policy

It is the case that the Euro, essentially a hybrid fixed exchange rate regime, engaged in by still sovereign states with fiscal autonomy, has come into being on the basis of a serious lack of understanding among politicians and policy makers about how exchange rates actually work, and how changes in them can affect competitiveness and thereby the level of economic activity, employment and so on in particular economies. The fundamentals are either unknown or are ignored in pursuit of the greater cause, that of 'building Europe'. This might appear to be an extravagant claim and so it is to be hoped that it will be vindicated by what follows in this section.

In a multi-currency environment, such as exists beyond the Euro, it is natural for each government to formulate and implement its own exchange rate policy: some would opt for a free floating rate and others for various forms of 'managed float' and some for the adoption of a fixed exchange rate regime against a stronger 'anchor' currency. This question can be a very highly charged political issue as monetary diplomacy between Japan and the United States over many decades has illustrated. Today, China's exchange rate policy is as widely criticised as that of Japan was in the 1980s and 1990s

Between 1947 and 1968/72 the Bretton Woods system of fixed exchange rates was adopted by most of the free world. Between 1979 and 1992 the Exchange Rate Mechanism of the European Monetary System attempted to stabilise exchange rates within the European Community. It must be said, however, that most of the major currency crises of the post-War world have afflicted currencies within fixed exchange rate regimes, for example Sterling in 1967, the Franc in 1969, the ERM generally in 1992. Suffice it to say that the ejection of Sterling from the ERM on 16th September 1992 was greeted in the City as the moment of economic liberation as the London stock market clearly announced.

And it is the case that as economic development, world trade and what is commonly called 'globalisation' have intensified, so many more countries have been drawn into the realms of the global financial markets, including of course, the foreign exchange market. This accounts for the fact that in the past twenty to thirty years currency crises have become more common and almost invariably have afflicted fixed exchange rate regimes.

For example, following the ERM crisis of 1992, which saw Sterling ejected from the System, a further crisis erupted the following year and this centred upon the French Franc and the Italian Lira. Further afield, the Mexican Peso suffered a major crisis in 1994/5, the Thai Baht, the Indonesian Rupiah, the Malaysian Ringgit and the Philippino Peso in 1997, the Russian Rouble in 1998. Some of the policy regimes were 'dirty floats' rather than absolutely fixed regimes but nonetheless, the evidence that fixed regimes share a common problem which allows them to function only in the short term appears to be overwhelming.

As the Euro may be regarded as a hybrid fixed exchange rate regime, it is extremely important to understand why such regimes are so prone to crisis and collapse. The vital point is that the processes which brought down Bretton Woods and the ERM have been at work *within the Euro* since the day of its invention and they therefore pose an ever greater danger to its survival. As will be described below the most important process of destabilisation concerns the relationship between two monetary concepts, the Nominal Exchange Rate and the Real Effective Exchange Rate (REER).

The most fundamental flaw in the 'reasoning' of the elite is for them to imagine that if you fix nominal exchange rates then you fix competitiveness. This idea, of fixing competitiveness is very probably the most dangerous and destructive economic delusion of the twentieth century – and sadly it endures into the present.

The fixing of competitiveness can never happen. It is precisely the great variations in the development of competitiveness that are now causing serious balance of payments and other problems within the Eurozone. Countries and regions which lose competitiveness within a currency union will also lose employment, output and investment as the option of devaluation is not open to them. This is the market at work but sadly few politicians are prepared to accept the evidence of this, even in those rare instances where they understand it.

We have been told endlessly, *ad infinitum, ad nauseam*, that the essential pre-condition for the creation and functioning of the Euro must be the 'irrevocable' and 'irreversible' fixing of exchange rates of the currencies which together make up the Single Currency. The use of these terms is not accidental, for they help the political class to persuade themselves and each other that they have exchange rate policy completely under their control and that this would in future prevent the manipulation of exchange rates, for example, by competitive devaluation.[2]

---

2 One has to question the use of such language, designed as it is to preclude rational discussion. In a democracy nothing is 'irrevocable' or 'irreversible' – not even the destruction of democracy itself. Policy can always be adjusted, changed and re-invented, for example, a new mandate from the electorate, the result of a popular election can never be predicted absolutely or gainsaid – as long as they are still allowed that is. So in these terms, this kind of language, so over-employed by the visionaries of the EU, seems intended to preclude, or to try to preclude, any future revision of their actions through the democratic process. Their language, worryingly, betrays their authoritarian instincts.

In this the creators and advocates of the Euro are totally wrong. It is not possible for politicians and bureaucrats to so completely control all monetary events or developments within the 'real' economy, that affect the evolution of exchange rates – this is out of their control, firstly because they cannot control the actions of other governments. In other words, the Eurozone has one supposed currency but cannot enforce a common exchange rate policy any more than it can enforce a common fiscal policy. It is precisely because of the relationship between the Nominal Exchange Rate, the Nominal Effective Exchange Rate and the REER, entities which must be carefully defined, that this situation exits. Claims to monetary omnipotence by the political class are most likely to make themselves, or rather their unfortunate constituents, the victims of the retribution of the financial markets.

The reasons for this are as follows: –

The nominal exchange rate is a bilateral (£/$, $/Euro) rate which is familiar to all travellers. The rate is a cash for cash figure but in a free or 'floating' market it is never constant but rather is constantly changing and this creates an inevitable sense of insecurity and doubt about the future trend of major exchange rates. This is because the foreign exchange market is for ever evaluating a myriad of economic, financial, political, economic and other news and events which affect the market perception of each economy and therefore also the value of its currency. The turnover of the market is about $3.2 trillion per day and this can and does create financially destructive volatility and this is why the market is so politically sensitive. It is precisely these characteristics of the market that makes the idea of fixed exchange rates appear so attractive.

Unlike the Nominal Exchange Rate, the Nominal Effective Exchange Rate and the Real Effective Exchange Rate are concerned not with cash transactions but rather are indices of a currency's *relative value*. Indices allow the relative performance of different currencies to be compared with some precision.

The Nominal Exchange Rate, the bilateral traded rate, is turned into the Nominal Effective Exchange Rate by averaging the exchange rates of the most traded currencies, against Sterling for example, and then weighting each one – giving it its statistical significance – according to the participation of each currency in Britain's trade. This gives an outline picture of the competitiveness or otherwise of the currency. The European Central Bank makes this calculation for the Euro daily, as do other financial authorities. The Deutsche Bundesbank evaluates the competitiveness of Germany on this basis among others.

However, the NER is rather narrowly based – the exchange rates, trade participation and sometimes trade balances – and so its usefulness here is also somewhat limited. However, when the NER is turned *'Real'* then it becomes of enormous significance, both in terms of both economic developments and economic policy. The nominal index is made 'real' by the inclusion of statistical elements that directly affect competitiveness such as inflation differentials, as measured by the Consumer Price Index, and other measures. In other words, the REER includes important measures of the performance of the 'real' economy, that is, the non-financial economy, and in this the industrial sector is of crucial importance. The REER is an immediate indicator of which countries are losing and which are gaining competitiveness.

The REER can also be calculated using other tests of competitiveness such as the trend of hourly earnings in industry, of labour productivity and also the relative movement of Unit Labour Costs. Unit Labour Costs are defined by the Organisation for Economic Cooperation and Development in the following term, 'ULCs can be calculated as the ratio of labour compensation to real GDP. It is also the equivalent of the ratio between labour compensation per labour input (per hour or per employee) worked and productivity'. In simple terms ULCs attempt to determine the labour cost of producing a unit of Gross Domestic Product.

What are the implications of all this? The economic meaning must be considered within an intensely political environment. In terms of competitiveness the movement of the REERs will immediately answer the question, 'which are the strongest economic performers and which are the weakest?' The answer to these questions are of vital importance, because the greater the divergence between the strong performers, Germany and the Netherlands and the weak performers, Italy, Greece, Spain, and Portugal, then the more likely it is that the system of fixed exchange rates will implode and collapse. Furthermore, the longer recognition of this reality is delayed, the more violent and destructive the final denouement will be as was clearly seen in the road to inevitable destruction of both the Bretton Woods system and more spectacularly, the ERM.

EUROPE NORTH AND SOUTH: UNIT LABOUR COSTS:2000 = 100

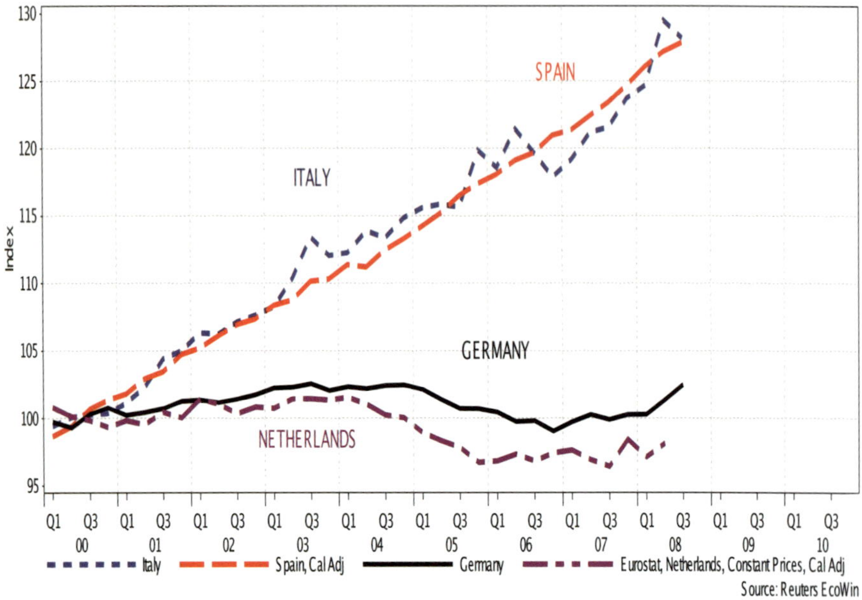

It is well worth repeating that simple inflation differentials have been perhaps the most lethal solvent of supposedly 'fixed' or 'irreversibly fixed' exchange rate regimes. Inflation differentials were very instrumental in bringing down the Bretton Woods system and then in wrecking the European Exchange Rate Mechanism in 1992. The ERM endured eight crises in its first ten years and the longer it went without subsequent exchange rate adjustment the more certain it was that it would fail.

As David F DeRosa has also pointed out, in the twenty years after 1979, the ERM, which we were told would bring greater financial stability '...suffered a total of eighteen realignments affecting fifty-six central rates'. There is no evidence at all to show that fixed exchange rate regimes do anything to assure stability. All the evidence is that the opposite is the case.

The evidence so far in the term of the Euro is entirely against the idea of its survival. The workings of the REER have produced the following divergent pattern of developments and the graph is no more or less than an indication of which countries will be overcome by crisis and which will come later. The following graph simply shows the extraordinarily divergent trend of competitiveness among the larger Euro economies: -

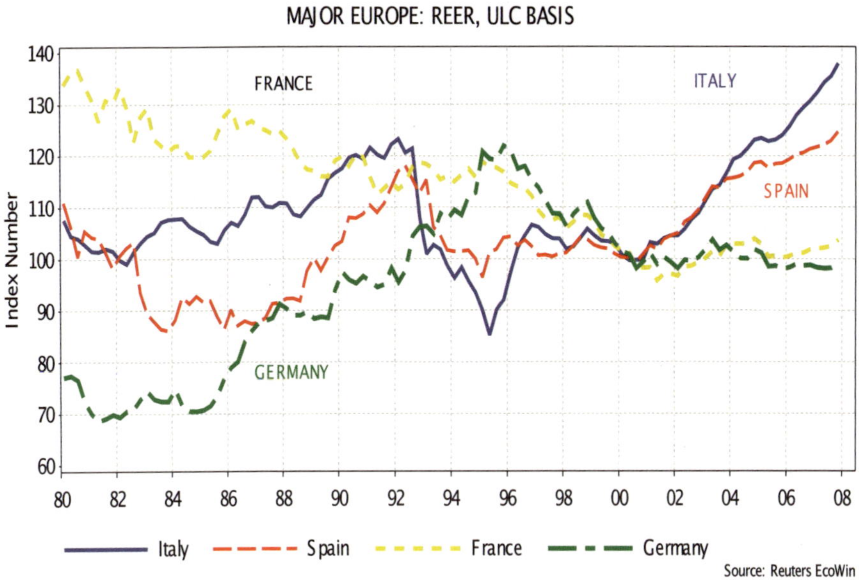

The inevitable consequence of this pattern of the gaining and losing of competitiveness within the single currency is that imbalances in EU trade and payments have already become unsustainable as will be demonstrated below. That is merely the first consequence of an ill-conceived and premature currency union; what follows is that production, jobs and investment will follow trade with inestimable implications for the 'ever-closer....union'.

In a free market with floating exchange rates, a market driven devaluation at least mitigates the loss of competitiveness, balance of payments deficits and the resulting accumulation of foreign debt. It must be stressed, once again, that exactly the same processes which acted in the 1950s and 1960s to wreck Bretton Woods and in the 1990s to wreck the ERM are at work *within the Euro* and that is why the danger to the survival of the currency is so severe when seen in economic and historical rather than in political or ideological terms. *Monetary Nemesis stalks the corridors of power in Brussels and Frankfurt.*

The position of the smaller economies such as Ireland and Greece was moving towards a situation of total un-sustainability from the very outset of the Single Currency in 2002.

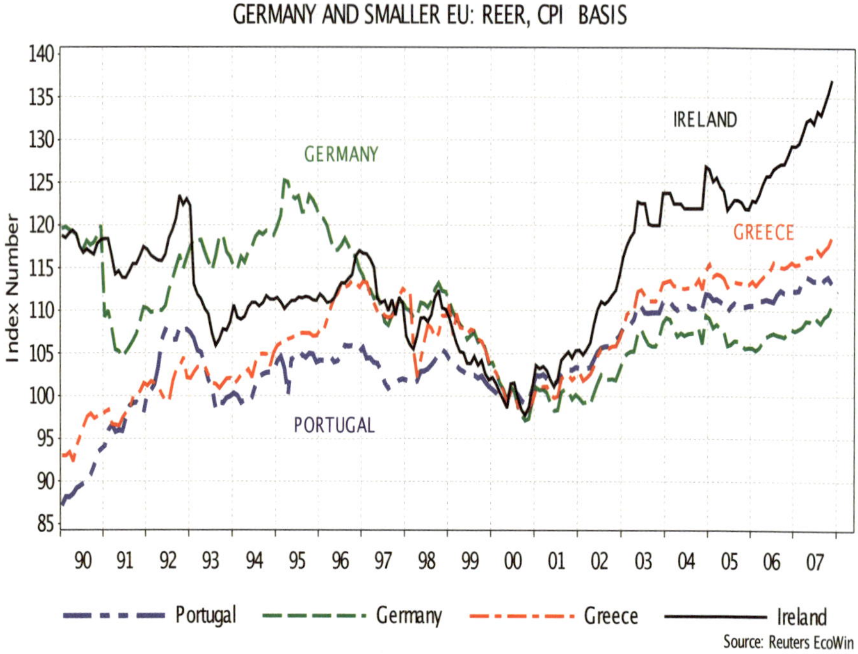

This is the case because a sustained loss of competiveness, such as Italy has endured, inevitably results in the deterioration of the trade and current account balances and the resulting deficits must be funded by the issuance of foreign debt, that is to say, government debt denominated in foreign currencies. This means that no matter how strict the programmes of fiscal retrenchment that are being forced upon the Mediterranean-Rim and other economies, the Euro militates against the correction of trade and current account deficits. It does not entirely preclude such an outcome – but it militates greatly against it, especially in the long term.

The problem is that too many countries are losing competitiveness against Europe's dominant economy, their largest trading partner and their strongest competitor. This situation cannot be overcome by the kind of fiscal over-kill that is being forced upon Greece and Ireland. This problem is monetary – but this can never be openly admitted.

Fiscal retrenchment, with all its attendant political dangers in somewhat volatile 'Latin' political cultures, may certainly lead to a reduction of the external borrowing requirement and this is a matter of fiscal policy. This can indeed produce a dramatic reduction of imports as has been seen in the Baltic States. What it will not do is to reduce the divergent trends of competitiveness as evidenced by the REER graphs shown previously and this is a matter of monetary policy – policy which seventeen sovereign States, incredibly, have handed over to a remote and secretive European Central Bank that has no public accountability and is beyond democratic control.

Perhaps the discussion may be encapsulated like this. The grandees of the EU consider that it is within their power to 'irrevocably fix' exchange rates, nominal exchange rates. What they have failed to comprehend is that fixing nominal exchange rates does not and cannot 'fix' competitiveness. Competitiveness is not reflected so much in the NER but is reflected, with deadly, indeed, disastrous implications for the Euro, in the relative development of the REERs.

The Hidden and Potentially Lethal Threat to the Euro: Germany's Exchange Rate Policy

The economic malaise in the Eurozone is commonly attributed to or 'blamed' upon the fiscal profligacy and administrative incompetence which are so representative of the political culture of the Mediterranean-Rim economies. This again emphasises the fiscal nature of the problem – they can hardly be accused of monetary incompetence because they are no longer in control of that policy. The 'blame' for monetary incompetence lies elsewhere. It must be asked: would the desperate predicament of Ireland have been anything like as bad as it is if The Republic, the Bank of Ireland, had had entire control of its monetary policy during the 'boom' years that awarded it the absurd title, The Celtic Tiger?

That blame lies entirely with the European Central Bank and those who created this disastrous situation ....the visionaries of the 'new' Europe, especially individuals such as Jacques Delors, Francois Mitterrand and Helmut Kohl. It had presided over an irrational regime in which countries with rapid growth, Ireland and Spain have been made to share a common interest rate policy with slow growing economies, Germany and the Netherlands. It is worse still: the European Central Bank has dictated a common exchange rate for Germany with the second largest current account surplus in the world and Spain with the second largest trade deficit in the world. How can this possibly be justified outside the asylum, or indeed *inside* the asylum?

Here the point should be made that while central banks covet their autonomy and independence, the Euro itself is a political construct, disliked by many central bank governors and economists – particularly those of the Deutsche Bundesbank. The decision to impose the Euro upon the EU was entirely political and economic and financial logic was always ignored. As indeed were the wishes of the German people who were not, of course, consulted about the loss of the Deutschemark, the most credible currency of the European Union.

It is now increasingly probable that faced with ruinous bills for the Euro bailouts, the German populace may now have to be consulted about the abandonment of the Euro and the restoration of the Deutschemark, a currency which never confronted that country with the problems and demands that it now faces.

Here it will be argued that the problem is not the fiscally profligate and politically incompetent and corrupt Greece or its Latin neighbours, the problem is the fiscally correct and ruthlessly competitive Germany. Germany is both the largest and by far the most powerful economy in Europe: it accounts for one fifth of the GDP of the 27 countries of the EU and more problematically, for some 28% of economic activity in the Eurozone. This means that the economic performance of Germany has an immediate and direct impact upon all other member states. If Germany were not such a colossus then the arguments that follow would not be so critical to the survival of the Euro.

A major problem with Germany has been and still is the structure of its economic growth, especially when compared with that of other major member economies and this is nothing new. Germany is overly dependent upon export led growth while domestically generated stimulus is typically weak, especially, again, in comparison with other EU economies.

As will be seen below, Germany's trade is overly concentrated upon the EU from which it derives substantial trade and current account surpluses. In other words, Europe's largest and strongest economy contributes very directly to the external deficits of her 'partners' and these deficits result directly to the growth of external debt. Debt has proved ruinous to Greece and Ireland and it is not 'contagion' that will make this much worse, it is the result of 'common' interest and exchange rate policies that have been pursued since the creation of the functioning Euro on 1st January 2002.

Put simply, the likes of Greece, Italy, Ireland, Spain and Portugal must borrow, incur external debt, in order to finance the trade and current account surpluses of Germany. Are we to believe that this is a credible or sustainable model of economic development?

This raises another issue: it is often asserted, once again *ad nauseam*, that Europe is moving towards 'ever-closer economic and political union'. One expression of this is the increasing intensification of regional trade and payments dependencies within the EU. The idea that an ever more intense trade dependencies within such a trading bloc is necessarily good, is very open to question. Economic history, and a modicum of common sense, suggests that the more diversified the pattern of world commerce then the less will be the vulnerability to regional failures and shocks. Is not this diversification simply 'globalisation' – a concept and reality that arouses suspicion and loathing in many continental countries, especially France?

The intensification of regional trade dependencies is not desirable – and it is the case that in the economies of Eastern Europe, dependence for both imports and exports from and to Germany has become actively dangerous. One aspect of this danger is that as regional trade dependencies become more intense, then so do Germany's trade and current account surpluses rise to ever more ruinous levels for her unfortunate EU 'partners'. Thus, the overwhelming industrial and commercial power of Germany, allied to the intensification of regional trade patterns has produced, not economic convergence and contentment but rather a pattern of trade and payments that is simply one sided and unsustainable. This point will be enlarged upon later.

It is indeed economically perverse that the Eurozone's largest and most powerful economy relies upon its weaker 'partners' for what little economic dynamism that it displays. For Germany there is a huge risk, that as its competitiveness produces ever larger trade surpluses with its financially sinking 'partners' – an eventual correction or collapse of this perverse economic arrangement would leave Germany herself bereft of any of its growth stimulus.

These characteristics of the German economy have been evident for decades. In the normally pointless processes of international economic summitry, be it the G7 or G8 or G20 or the OECD or the Ecofin meetings of the EU, the blame for the ills of the world economy frequently falls upon the United States for spending too much and Germany for spending too little. French politicians, for example, the very able Economics Minister, Christine Lagard, have been particularly vociferous in their criticism of Germany's anomalous state, especially because it is seen to result from the deliberate conduct of German economic policy.

When the Euro was founded in 1999, it was fondly assumed that with Germany's exchange rate 'irrevocably fixed', then there would be no more periodic crises such as those which repeatedly afflicted the ERM between 1979 and 1992. The ruling elite, now in total control, could sit back smugly anticipating economic convergence and the facilitation of political union, however ill-defined this concept is and no matter how unwanted.

It was never going to happen like this. Rather, German exchange rate policy, within the Euro, represents the most lethal danger to the survivability of the Single Currency. The fundamental reason for this is stark in its simplicity.

The idea of 'irrevocably fixing' the value of the Deutschemark turned history on its head and this single act absolutely guaranteed economic and financial instability for the future. It is worth remembering that during the Bretton Woods era and then that of the ERM the DMark *was only ever revalued and never devalued.* During the troubled years of the ERM, currency crises invariably resulted in demands for the revaluation of the DMark – it could never, of course, be called a devaluation of the Franc – such is the absurdity of currency jingoism.

Thus, all the historical experience indicated that preventing future revaluations of the DMark would cause major problems. The DMark would simply become too competitive. This danger has been enormously increased by the conduct of German exchange rate policy. In very marked contrast to the previous conduct of German policy, the policies implemented during the era of the Euro have changed with very serious implications for the Single Currency. The German monetary authorities, having been denied any discretion over the nominal exchange rate of the DMark, have resorted to an extremely successful strategy to ensure the future competitiveness of Germany, and thus to sustain its trade and current account surpluses within the Euro.

The new German exchange rate policy is radical, to bring about the devaluation of the Real Effective Exchange Rate itself.

Germany's exchange rate policy is founded upon the manipulation of those elements that determine the direction of the REER, elements that will determine whether Germany either gains or loses competitiveness. This centres upon the labour market, the structure of which was greatly influenced by the concept of the 'social-market economy', the brainchild of Dr Ludwig Erhard, the first Economics Minister of the Federal Republic and later its Chancellor, 1963-1966.

Erhard wished to avoid the polarization of economic forces and so a tripartite labour market structure emerged involving the trade unions, the employers and the State itself. This tri-partite structure certainly helped to avoid any possible repeat of the emergence of deep social, economic and political divisions which emerged after the First World War. The policy was largely successful as Germany avoided the debilitating conflicts that plagued the labour markets of the UK and other countries at this time. The orderly labour market greatly contributed to the emergence and preservation of Germany's quite remarkable international competitiveness and its success in developing overseas trade. This domestic achievement was complemented by the Bretton Woods system of fixed exchange rates which increasingly *undervalued* the DMark, thus contributing to Germany's 'economic miracle'.

The competitive position of Germany suffered a severe setback as the result of another failed monetary experiment, that of the monetary union of the Federal Republic and the German Democratic Republic in November 1990. The ruling elite naturally gained and learned nothing from this disastrous experiment. The so-called 'black-market' dictated an exchange rate of between 4 and 6 East German Ostmarks to the DMark, but monetary union, for political reasons, was pushed through at an exchange rate of 1 Ostmark for 1 DMark. This exchange rate resulted in the summary ruination of the GDR economy, such as it was, creating the necessity for massive fiscal transfers from West to East. The Euro has had a similar result, not summary ruination but rather, death by a thousand cuts for Germany's competitors. The German nation was quite prepared to pay an enormous price for reunification: it is now being asked to pay an inestimable sum to sustain the Euro. The political will to do this is increasingly in doubt.

The unification of the German labour market severely diluted the strong competitive position that had been painstakingly built-up in the Federal Republic because East German labour productivity was accurately reflected in the black-market exchange rate: it amounted at best to one quarter of the productivity of West German workers. It was natural that with monetary union, Western price levels were imposed upon East Germany – the labour unions responded by demanding equal pay to compensate. The East German economy could not possibly survive such a grossly over-valued exchange rate and aggressive wage demands.

The collapse of East German economic activity was directly reflected in the balance of payments and unified Germany recorded current account deficits in 1991 and 1992, and the respective position of the two Germanies is reflected in the figures presented in the following table: -

Germany East and West: Trade Balances

	Billion DM			% GDP		
Year	Germany	West	East	Germany	West	East
1990	-	141.9	-	-	5.9	-
1991	-6.8	152.1	-159.0	-0.2	5.6	-78.5
1992	-7.7	178.0	-194.8	-0.2	6.5	-74.9
1993	5.6	210.2	-204.5	0.2	7.2	-64.2
1994	10.7	224.2	-213.4	0.3	7.4	-58.0
1995	22.7	-	-	0.6	-	-
1996	37.2	-	-	1.0	-	-
1997	50.1	-	-	1.4	-	-
1998	57.4	-	-	1.5	-	-
1999	37.6	-	-	1.0	-	-
2000	15.3	-	-	0.4	-	-

(Source: European Commission, European Economy, Economic Papers, Germany's Growth Performance in the 1990s, Paper No. 170, May 2002)

The deficits were due entirely to the collapse of production in the GDR and the disintegration of its balance of payments, the FRG always remained in substantial surplus but this was overwhelmed by the sheer size of the Eastern deficit which reached a staggering 78.5% of GDP in 1991. The return to surplus in 1993 was due entirely to the extraordinary efforts of the FRG's export sector.

In response to these economic threats to the established German order, the 'social partners' of the social-market economy, the unions, employers and the government, negotiated the *'Bundnis Fur Arbeit'* – the Compact for Work. This 'solidarity pact' was based upon the idea that the employers would try to preserve employment and the unions would accept the containment of wage demands and more flexible working practices. And it is the legacy of this arrangement of 1996 that now threatens the survivability of the single currency.

There have been subsequent modifications of the German labour model, for example, the Hartz Reforms of 2002. However, there is no doubt that what has come to be known as the Active Labour Market Policy has been of enormous importance for the development of the German labour market. The outstanding point is that the State is very actively engaged in the preservation of employment and the remarkable sophistication of the German labour force. The benefits of this approach were seen during the years of the 'credit crunch' when unemployment was contained through the holding of 'mini-jobs' and widespread short time working, *Kurzarbeit*. Chancellor Merkel has said that the preservation of jobs, albeit often with substantial government subsidies, amounts to a 'minor miracle'.

Germany's exchange rate policy is exercised through the labour market and the management of inflation. It has been noted that inflation differentials have been the most destructive solvent of 'fixed' exchange rate regimes because differentials so immediately affect relative competitiveness. Membership of the Euro was made conditional under the terms of the Maastricht Criteria these included the provision that a country should not have an inflation rate any more than 1.5% higher than the average of the three best performing economies. There is no doubt that there was a dramatic reduction of inflation differentials in preparation for the introduction of the currency as the following graph illustrates: –

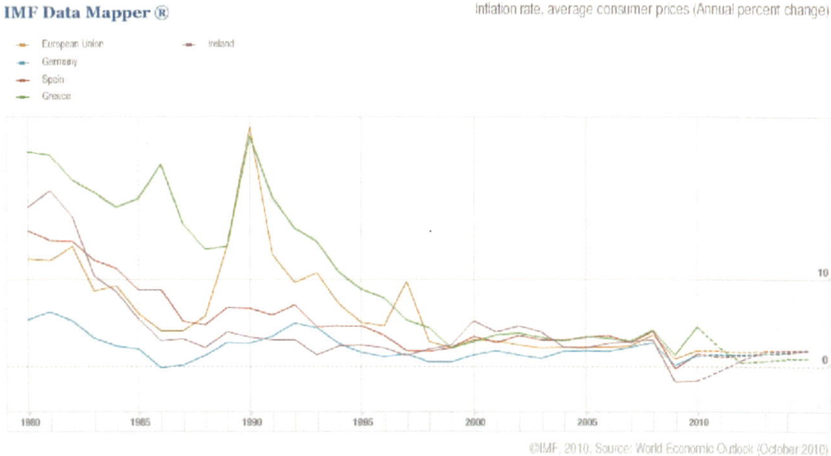

It was this closing of inflation differentials which subsequently allowed interest rates to inappropriately low levels in Spain, Ireland, Greece and other countries. This in turn added to the creation of the 'bubble economy' of the last decade.

The time scale given in this graph is illustrative and a more complete statistical account may be found towards the end of this publication in the Statistical Appendix.

Let us consider the meaning of these figures – and the first point to be made is that they come from an unimpeachable source, the International Monetary Fund. The IMF, and other agencies such as the OECD, the World Bank and the Bank for International Settlements all stand in marked contrast to Eurostat – the statistical office of the European Union. This organisation, like so many presided over by the grandees of Brussels, has been tainted by scandal and corruption which inevitably casts doubt upon the integrity of its statistical work.

In response to revelations of blatant fraud, nepotism and corruption leading to the theft of millions of taxpayers Euros, it was no surprise to learn that the then EU President, that fearless advocate of public probity, Romano Prodi, quickly announced that there were no grounds for any resignations among 'senior' personnel. That is to say, among failed Commissioners and their corrupt acolytes. The career of Commissioner Pedro Solbes, having had direct responsibility for the management of Eurostat, was saved only by the 'fact' of his claimed ignorance of the corrupt goings on in his own bureaucratic fiefdom![3]

To return to the Graph – high inflation economies lose competitiveness and low inflation economies gain. The first point to be made about these figures is that since the introduction of the Euro in 2002, Germany's inflation rate has only once been above that of the Eurozone average and similarly, that of Italy has never been below that average and Spain shares that experience. These wide inflation differentials do not by themselves determine the course of international competitiveness but they are a very important early warning signal. As we have noted, these differentials caused repeated havoc within the ERM, always resulting in the revaluation of the low inflation DMark.

The Euro makes such an outcome, devaluation and revaluation, impossible but nevertheless, the Real Effective Exchange Rate of the DMark is either being devalued or is out-performing those of its leading competitors. The gains and losses of competitiveness are chronic, cumulative processes which might seem unimportant in the initial stages: however the experience of the ERM tells us unambiguously that the longer these processes go on the more severe will become the strains within the system, the Euro. After the build up of such pressures within the ERM over a five year period, the system imploded in 1992.

The statistical evidence indicating the remarkable success of Germany's exchange rate policy is set out in the following Table. The figures, like those for inflation, are provided by the IMF in its twice yearly publication, *World Economic Outlook*. These figures are an updated version of the statistics that I employed in a Bruges Group publication, *Is the Euro Sustainable?* which was published in 2009. These figures give a very clear indication of changes in relative competitiveness and are based upon movements in earnings, productivity and Unit Labour Costs.

3. But this is not all. When it was revealed that the Greek authorities had been providing 'fraudulent' financial statistics in an effort to conceal the full extent of their fiscal deficits, the Brussels Commission indulged itself in a particularly display of sanctimonious cant. An EU 'source' stated that 'infringement procedures' would be initiated '....because providing timely and reliable statistics is an obligation under EU law and they have failed in their obligation'. The only difference is that of political expediency by the Greek establishment and outright corruption in Brussels. The former evidently matters, the latter does not.

Eurozone: Labour Market Indicators of Competitiveness

	92-01*	02-11*	2002	2003	2004	2005	2006	2007	2008	2009
EU CPI*+	2.3	-	2.3	2.1	2.2	2.2	2.2	2.1	3.3	0.3
Earnings**										
Advanced	3.9	3.0	4.0	4.9	2.1	3.3	2.8	3.6	3.2	2.5
Eurozone	3.6	2.9	3.6	3.1	2.7	3.1	3.1	3.3	3.5	2.4
Germany	4.3	2.2	2.4	2.5	0.8	2.2	2.8	2.7	2.7	4.3
France	3.7	3.1	4.2	2.4	4.9	3.6	3.5	3.8	3.0	1.2
Italy	3.6	3.1	3.3	3.3	3.2	4.6	3.0	2.9	4.2	2.2
Spain	4.6	3.8	4.9	4.9	3.3	4.3	4.1	3.7	4.8	5.0
USA	3.7	3.4	5.5	8.0	0.8	3.3	2.0	3.3	4.0	5.2
Japan	1.8	0.0	-1.3	1.0	0.4	1.3	0.4	0.0	1.5	-1.3
UK	4.7	3.2	3.5	3.6	3.6	3.7	5.1	3.5	3.0	1.7
Productivity+										
Advanced	3.3	2.5	4.3	4.7	3.4	3.9	2.4	2.9	-0.7	-2.4
Eurozone	3.4	1.5	1.3	2.8	3.1	3.4	3.2	2.2	-0.2	-4.7
Germany	3.2	2.2	0.9	3.9	4.1	5.3	6.5	3.1	-0.1	-9.8
France	4.4	1.8	3.0	4.3	4.1	5.0	3.2	2.7	-0.8	-6.5
Italy	1.5	-0.2	-0.8	-0.6	1.0	0.6	0.5	0.4	-0.9	-2.4
Spain	4.2	1.5	2.2	2.2	1.6	1.8	1.3	-0.3	-2.0	2.1
USA	3.9	3.3	6.9	6.3	2.3	4.7	0.8	3.4	-0.7	2.0
Japan	1.4	0.5	3.7	5.1	4.5	1.9	2.7	2.1	-3.9	-15.8
UK	3.0	2.6	2.5	5.2	6.6	4.8	2.9	3.7	0.1	-4.7
ULC										
Advanced	0.6	0.5	-0.3	0.3	-1.3	-0.5	0.4	0.2	4.1	5.8
Eurozone	0.8	1.3	2.3	0.3	-0.3	-0.2	-0.1	1.1	3.7	7.5
Germany	1.1	0.0	1.5	-1.3	-3.1	-2.9	-3.5	-0.4	2.8	15.6
France	-0.7	1.3	1.1	-1.8	0.8	-1.3	0.5	1.1	3.8	8.1
Italy	2.0	3.2	4.1	3.9	2.2	3.9	2.5	2.5	5.2	4.7
Spain	0.5	2.2	2.7	2.7	1.6	2.5	2.8	4.1	6.9	2.8
USA	-0.2	0.1	-1.3	1.6	-1.4	-1.3	1.2	-0.1	4.7	3.1
Japan	0.3	-0.5	-4.8	-3.9	-4.0	-0.6	-2.2	-2.1	5.6	17.3
UK	1.6	0.7	1.0	-1.5	-2.8	-1.1	2.2	-0.3	2.9	6.8

* Annual averages **Hourly earnings. +Labour productivity, measured as the ratio of hourly compensation to unit labour costs.*+ Consumer Price Index
(Source: IMF, *World Economic Outlook*, October 2010)

Germany's relatively low inflation rate is reflected in the highly disciplined behaviour of wages rates which in turn indicate a very slow increase in 'real' wages, that is wage rates adjusted for inflation. This slow growth is one extremely important cause of the weak growth of domestic demand, a factor which contributes greatly to the trade and current account surpluses. In terms of the movement of hourly wage rates, it is clear that Germany has improved its competitiveness against two of its most important Eurozone industrial competitors, France and Italy.

A somewhat similar trend of events is seen in terms of productivity, although in this case France has performed relatively well in the same period. However, Italy has actually recorded negative productivity growth in some years meaning that over the course of the last decade, Italy has achieved no gains in productivity at all, again with serious implications for that country's competitiveness. The IMF attributes this very poor performance to a deficiency in fixed investment, especially in industry and manufacturing. How could it be otherwise? If competitiveness is lost and profit margins squeezed then how could we expect investment to expand – or even to be sustained? This situation has been described by one Italian economist as being tantamount to 'the de-industrialisation of Italy'.

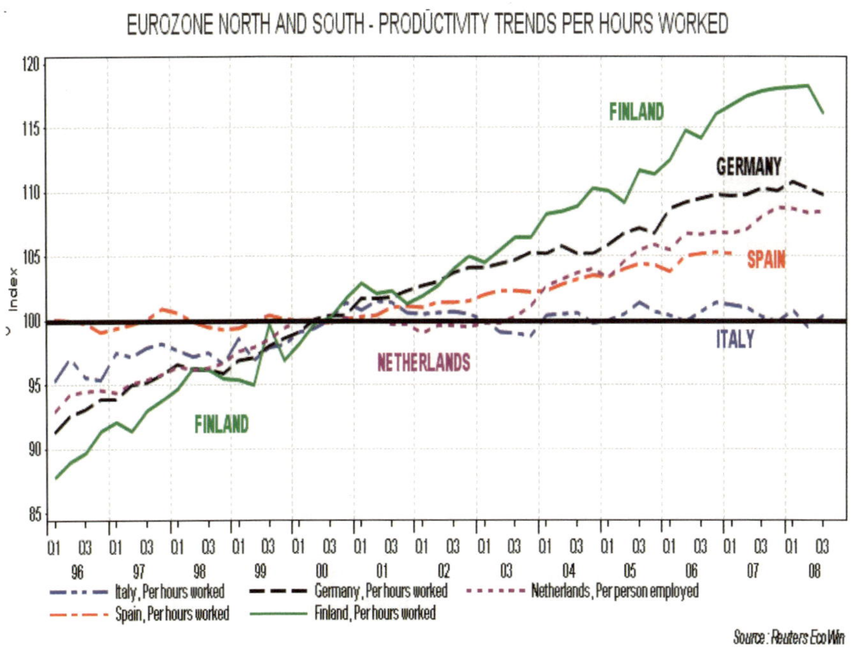

EUROPE NORTH AND SOUTH: UNIT LABOUR COSTS:2000 = 100

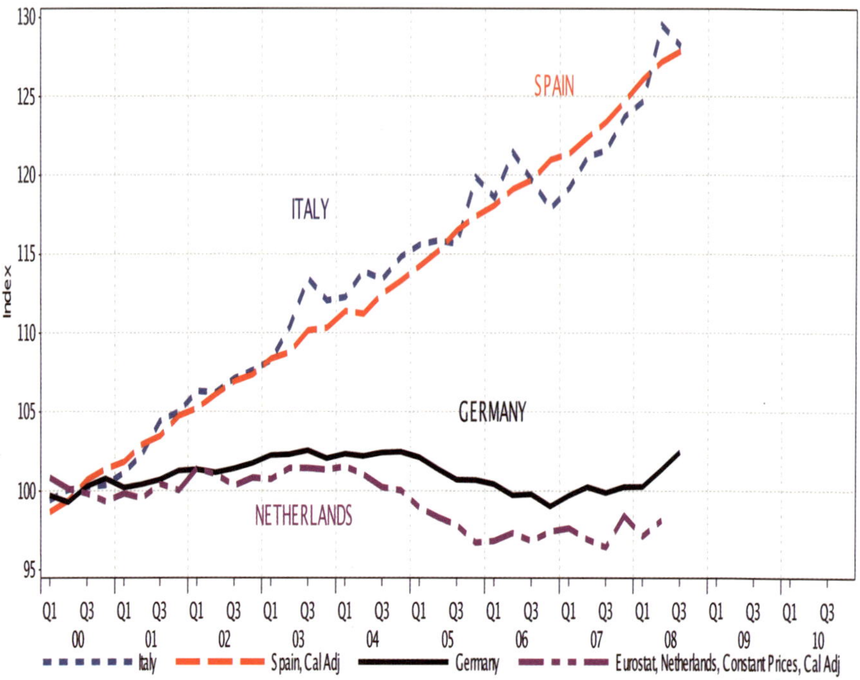

Source: Reuters EcoWin

This grim situation has prompted intermittent debate in Italy's political and economic circles about the desirability or not of that country remaining within the Eurozone – whatever fatuous noises Trichet might make on this issue. The problem then is that this debate is now a matter of concern to German economists and politicians.

Finally, the movement of relative Unit Labour Costs (ULCs) is of very great importance. The Organisation for Economic Cooperation and Development states that ULCs '...measure the average cost of labour per unit of output and are calculated as the ratio of total labour costs to real output'. A rise in ULCs implies greater rewards to labour but if this rise is greater than the growth of productivity, then a loss of competitiveness is implied. The most striking fact to emerge from these figures is the subdued trend of ULCs in Germany. Of course, this is reflected in the Eurozone figures but once again, the divergent performances of Germany and Italy illustrate clearly enough the extent of the gains and losses of competitiveness within the Eurozone. This is what will make the Euro ever more difficult to live with.

The statistical evidence is as worrying as it is complete. Is there a single advocate of the Euro who can question either the veracity or the implications of this evidence? Once again, the IMF can illustrate, in statistical terms the impact of these developments for the development of Real Effective Exchange Rates: –

Euroland and Beyond: The Movement of Real Effective Exchange Rates

2000 = 100	2002	2003	2004	2005	2006	2007	2008	2009
Euroland	105.6	119.7	125.7	124.2	123.8	129.1	138.5	139.8
Germany	101.1	105.4	105.5	102.1	99.0	100.6	101.4	100.9
France	100.4	103.4	106.5	105.7	107.3	110.1	112.2	109.7
Italy	106.1	118.0	124.5	127.5	129.2	133.8	143.0	151.4
Spain	103.6	110.1	114.6	118.5	122.0	127.9	124.4	138.7
Netherlands	105.3	112.5	113.8	111.7	111.4	113.6	118.5	121.3
Belgium	103.8	109.3	109.8	110.0	112.8	114.1	116.4	118.0
Austria	101.1	105.0	106.9	107.2	104.7	104.5	104.7	103.0
Finland	98.4	100.6	101.5	101.2	96.9	93.6	97.5	110.0
Greece	118.9	121.6	121.6	116.7	120.9	123.4	116.0	122.7
Portugal	102.1	104.7	107.2	109.8	111.8	109.5	110.9	108.7
Ireland	91.4	100.4	104.6	111.0	109.5	107.1	112.5	102.2
Luxembourg	103.0	106.8	106.8	107.2	109.9	110.7	112.2	113.4
United States	101.6	93.0	86.3	83.9	84.2	81.0	77.4	81.4
Japan	84.9	78.4	76.5	70.5	64.5	59.3	65.8	71.3

(Source: IMF, *World Economic Outlook*, October 2010, Statistical Appendix)

The evidence is devastating: while the REER of the Eurozone has risen by 39.8% since the start of the Index, the REER of Germany has remained flat and Italy's Index has risen by a ruinous 51.4%. Really, it is precisely the case that the figures speak for themselves. This can hardly be described as 'economic convergence' and represents a serious and apparently insoluble problem for those countries which have lost competitiveness during the era of the Euro.

It is hardly surprising that political figures such as Christine Lagarde have complained that the increasingly serious imbalances within the Euro are the result of German policy. Some commentators have called this the new mercantilism. The wider consequences of these divergent trends of competitiveness are seen most plainly in the trend of industrial production which hugely favours Germany which produces far more than it can consume and therefore exports to other European nations. One is again reminded of the idea of the de-industrialisation of Italy.

ITALY, GERMANY AND EUROLAND: INDUSTRIAL PRODUCTION

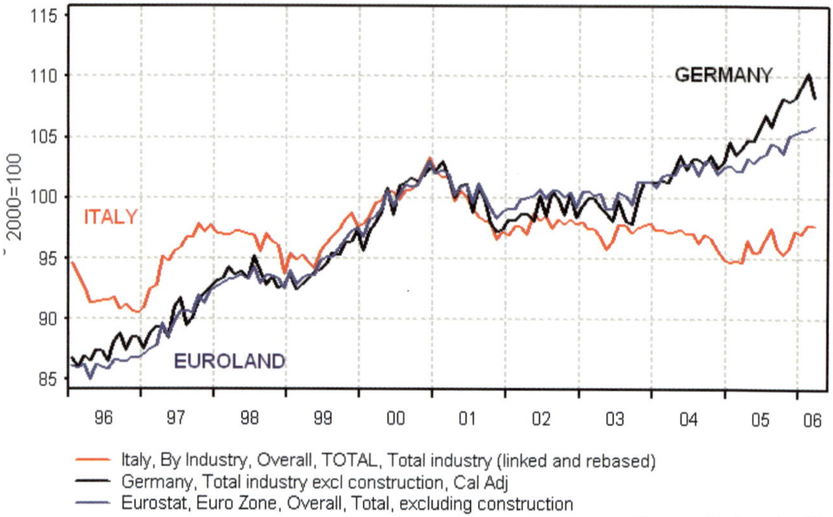

Source: Reuters EcoWin

Germany: The Pattern of Trade and Payments

Germany, according to the World Trade Organisation, was second only to China in 2008 as an exporting economy, the United States being third. Similarly, Germany, according to the IMF, had the second largest current account surplus after China with Japan being in third place. Current account balances are frequently measured as a percentage of GDP and China led with a surplus of 9.98% of GDP followed by Germany at 6.68% and Japan in third place with a more modest 3.19%.

This might at first sight seem to be good news, a reconstituted Germany, showing herself to be integrated into the 'globalising' world economy and reaping the rewards for her management of a highly disciplined labour market and remarkably successful export economy. Sadly, the reality is very different: Germany's outstanding commercial success is a very parochial affair, Germany is far too dependent upon the EU markets both for its export success and for its massive trade and current account surpluses. The movement of the REERs has obviously contributed to this situation which obliges Germany's trading 'partners' to incur external debt in order to finance Germany's trade and current account surpluses. This is stranger than economic fiction.

This over-dependence is well illustrated in the following table: –

Germany: Major Export Markets

	2007	2008	2009
Total Exports in billions of Euro	965.2	984.1	803.4
As % of Total Exports	2007	2008	2009
European Countries	75.2	74.4	73.8
European Union 27	64.6	63.2	63.2
Eurozone 16	43.6	42.6	43.3
Other European	10.6	11.2	10.5
Non-European Countries	24.5	25.3	26.6
Africa	0.1	1.9	2.1
America	10.4	10.3	9.0
United States	7.5	7.2	6.6
Asia	11.5	12.2	13.8
Middle East	2.4	2.7	2.9

Japan	1.3	1.2	1.3
China	3.0	3.4	4.5
Oceania and Polar Regions	0.7	0.7	0.8

(Source: Deutsche Bundesbank, Monthly Report, June 2010)

The contrast between Germany's participation in the trade of Europe, Asia and the United States appears quite extraordinary. Asia has dominated global economic growth and is steadily eroding the relative standing of Europe in world export markets. It is the case that in the post-war period world trade has tended to grow more rapidly than output, meaning that exports have been a major engine of economic growth. Within this context, Europe's market share has declined, although, led by Germany it remains by far the most export dependent region of the world economy. In its most recent *World Economic Outlook*, the IMF estimated that the population of the Eurozone amounted to just 4.8% of the world population. However, this region generated no less than 15.2% of world GDP and much more worryingly, 28.8% of world exports.

In these terms Germany's very high level of export dependency upon Europe, accounting for about three quarters of her exports, appears to be quite extraordinary as does the relatively low level of exports to the United States. This is the more extraordinary given the sophistication of German exports, including the high end of the car market.

Once again, the figures emphasise just how anomalous Germany's position is. As has been noted, in 2007 some 75.2% of German exports were consigned to the European market, and 43.6% to the Eurozone economies. In the same year exports to France accounted for 9.4%, while those to the United States, the world's largest importer by far, amounted to a mere 6.9%. Given that the US market is some five times larger than that of France and is a very open one, it seems extraordinary that France's import bill exceeds that of the US by getting on for €20 billion.

Reviewing these extraordinary figures, it comes as no surprise to learn that Germany's substantial trade and current account surpluses are centred almost entirely upon Europe, once again illustrating the very unequal economic relationship between these two entities.

Germany: Regional Trade Balances

Euro Billions	2007	2008	2009
Total Exports	965.2	984.1	803.4
Total Imports	769.8	805.8	667.3
Balance	195.3	178.2	136.0
European Countries	2007	2008	2009
Exports	726.5	733.0	593.0
Imports	541.6	567.0	475.4
Balance	184.8	166.0	117.6
EU Members Exports	623.8	622.6	508.3
Imports	449.6	460.8	392.6
Balance	174.1	161.7	115.7
Eurozone 16 Exports	421.5	419.5	347.9
Imports	307.1	315.0	268.2
Balance	114.3	104.5	79.7
Austria Exports	52.8	54.6	48.2
Imports	32.0	33.1	29.0
Balance	20.7	21.5	19.1
Belgium Exports*	55.3	55.2	46.8
Imports	39.4	39.9	32.0
Balance	15.9	15.2	14.7
France Exports	91.6	93.7	81.9
Imports	62.8	63.3	54.5
Balance	28.7	30.3	27.3
Italy Exports	64.4	62.0	51.0
Imports	44.6	46.8	39.6
Balance	19.8	15.1	11.3
Netherlands Exports	62.9	65.7	54.1
Imports	61.9	67.9	58.0
Balance	0.9	-2.1	-3.9
Spain Exports	47.6	42.6	31.2

Imports	20.6	20.7	19.2
Balance	26.9	21.9	12.0
Other EU Exports	202.6	203.0	160.4
Imports	142.5	145.8	124.4
Balance	59.7	57.2	36.0
United Kingdom Exports	69.7	64.1	53.1
Imports	41.9	41.6	33.1
Balance	27.7	22.5	19.9
Other European Exports	102.6	110.4	84.6
Imports	91.9	106.1	82.7
Balance	10.7	4.2	1.8
Non European Countries Exports	237.1	249.1	213.8
Imports	227.5	238.0	197.9
Balance	9.5	11.1	15.9
Africa Exports	17.5	19.6	17.2
Imports	16.4	20.6	14.2
Balance	1.1	-1.0	2.9
America Exports	100.7	101.8	77.9
Imports	71.2	73.8	60.9
Balance	29.4	27.9	16.9
United States Exports	73.2	71.4	53.8
Imports	45.9	46.4	39.9
Balance	27.3	24.9	13.9
Asia Exports	111.6	120.1	111.6
Imports	136.4	140.5	120.0
Balance	-24.7	-20.4	-8.4
Middle East Exports	23.7	27.4	23.3
Imports	6.4	7.9	5.4
Balance	17.2	19.5	17.8
Japan Exports	13.0	12.7	10.7
Imports	24.3	23.1	18.1
Balance	-11.3	-10.3	-7.3

China Exports	29.9	34.0	36.4
Imports	56.4	60.8	55.4
Balance	-26.5	-26.7	-18.9
Asia South East Emerging Exports	32.2	32.5	28.3
Imports	35.3	33.1	27.7
Balance	-3.0	-0.5	0.5
Oceania, Polar Regions Exports	7.1	7.5	7.0
Imports	3.4	2.9	2.7
Balance	3.6	4.6	4.3

*Includes Luxemburg.
(Source: Bundesbank, Monthly Report, June 2010, Statistical Section)

The pattern of the trade and current account balances is as disturbing as the pattern of trade itself. Of the total trade surplus of €195.3 billion in 2007, that with the European countries amounted to €184.8 billion, equivalent to 94.6% , with the EU, 89.1% and with the Eurozone, 58.5%. The trade surplus with the US was insignificant in comparison.

It has been noted that Europe is the most export dependent economic region of the world economy. In its most recent *World Economic Outlook*, the IMF estimated that the population of the Eurozone amounted to just 4.8% of the world population. However, this region generated no less than 15.2% of world GDP and much more worryingly, 28.8% of world exports. This proportion is already in steep decline as the epicentre of world production shifts from the Atlantic to the Pacific and from Europe to Asia.

Despite these extraordinary figures, the EU is now in current account deficit as is seen in the following IMF provided graph. That the world's most export dependent region should be in deficit is very worrying but is not an issue which the elite would care to trouble themselves with. And the IMF projections of the recovery of the EU position is such as to cause Dr Pangloss severe embarrassment – from where exactly is this recovery coming from? There is more likely to be an utter collapse of domestic demand in the nations of the 'new' currency era.

The point then is that if each EU economy were free to determine its own exchange rate, and then there is no doubt at all countries such as Italy and France would have opted for a mild devaluation. But as it is, they are chained to an essentially German exchange rate with which makes their survival as exporting economies increasingly problematical. This becomes ever more the case when the Euro appreciates against the US dollar and other currencies because the burden of over-valuation falls, not upon Germany but rather upon her helpless monetary captives.

The chart indicates the obvious fragility of Eastern and Central Europe.

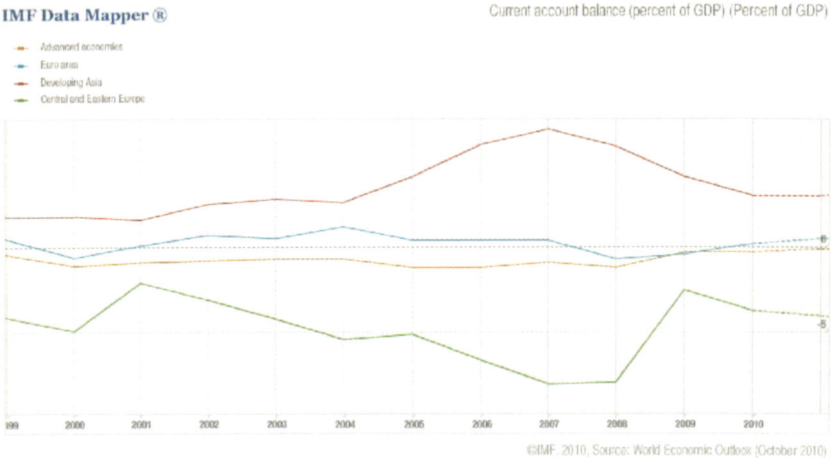

As the following chart makes very clear, among the major economies of the EU and Eurozone, Germany has attained a hugely dominant position and it is very difficult to see how this can be reversed to achieve a more balances pattern of trade and payments within the bloc. This means that countries such as Spain and Italy will have to continue to fund their current account deficits by increasing their external debt.

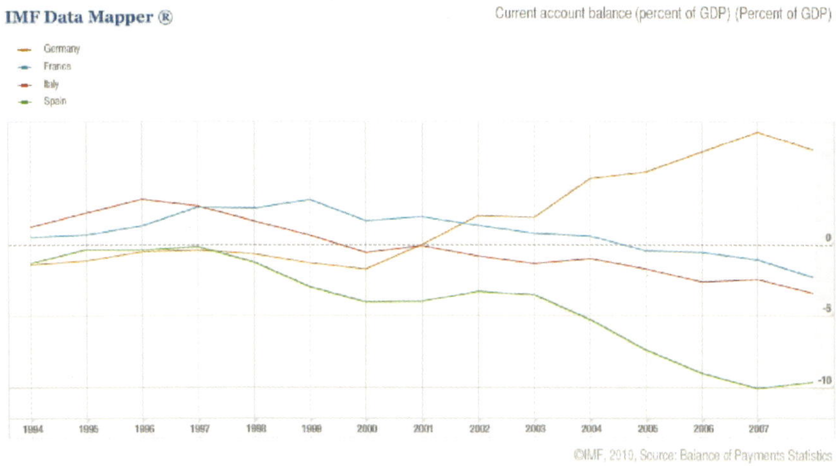

The imbalances among the major economies are imitated also by the smaller players as the following chart makes clear.

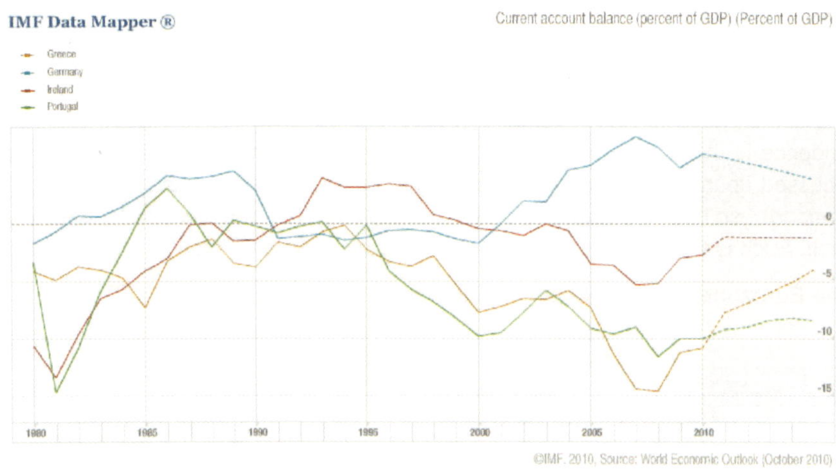

The chart includes the IMF's assessment of the immediate prospects and these at best amount to a stabilisation of current account positions and most certainly not any notion of a correction of these serous imbalances.

The following chart indicates clearly enough the divergent paths of the payments positions of the major players in Europe. The simple fact is that Germany's dollar denominated surplus has simply exploded since 2002... the introduction of the functioning Euro.

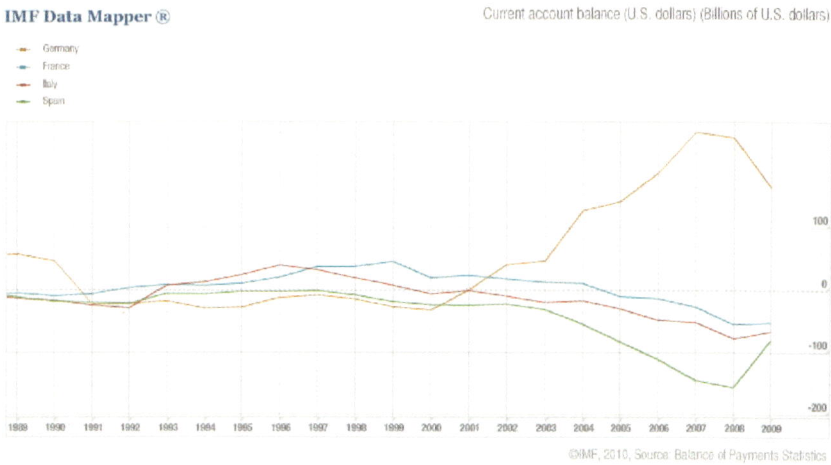

The IMF is not very optimistic about the fate of individual EU nations, apart from Germany. To find any comfort at all in the prospects for the future, it is necessary to find some cause for the reversal of the recent workings of the REER. But what evidence is there for such a correction? Policy responses to date have not been focussed upon real economic correction but merely the suppression of aggregate demand... so it is the symptoms of the disease that are treated and not the disease itself. Such is the economic management of the European 'Union'.

The Eurozone: Current Account Balances

	2002	2003	2004	2005	2006	2007	2008	2009
Euro Area US $ Bn.	47.9	42.9	116.9	45.3	47.6	47.3	-106.0	-43.8
Euro Area As % GDP	0.7	0.5	1.2	0.4	0.4	0.4	-0.8	-0.4
Germany	2.0	1.9	4.7	5.1	6.5	7.6	6.7	4.8
France	1.4	0.8	0.6	-0.4	-0.5	-1.0	-2.3	-1.5
Italy	-0.8	-1.3	-0.9	-1.7	-2.6	-2.4	-3.4	-3.4
Spain	-3.3	-3.5	-5.3	-7.4	-9.0	-10.0	-9.6	-5.1

Netherlands	2.5	5.5	7.5	7.3	9.3	8.7	4.8	5.2
Belgium	4.6	4.1	3.5	2.6	2.0	2.2	-2.5	-0.3
Greece	-6.5	-6.5	-5.8	-7.5	-11.3	-14.4	-14.6	-11.2
Austria	2.7	1.7	2.1	2.0	2.8	3.1	3.5	1.4
Portugal	-8.1	-6.1	-7.6	-9.5	-10.0	-9.4	-12.1	-10.1
Finland	8.8	5.2	6.6	3.6	4.6	4.2	3.0	1.4
Ireland	-1.0	0.0	-0.6	-3.5	-3.6	-5.3	-5.2	-2.9
Slovakia	-7.9	-5.9	-7.8	-8.5	-7.8	-5.3	-6.5	-3.2
Slovenia	1.1	-0.8	-2.7	-1.7	-2.5	-4.8	-6.2	-0.3
Luxembourg	10.5	8.1	11.9	11.0	10.3	9.7	5.3	5.7
Cyprus	-3.7	-2.2	-5.0	-5.9	-7.0	-11.7	-17.7	-9.3
Malta	2.5	-3.1	-6.0	-8.8	-9.2	-6.2	-5.4	-3.9

(Source: IMF, *World Economic Outlook*, October 2010)

One point to be made about this situation is that the Maastricht Criteria for membership of the Euro made no reference at all to the trade and current account positions of the aspiring member states. It seems incredible that countries such as Portugal and Greece, exhibiting serious current account problems in 2002, should have been admitted at all. It seems equally perverse that Slovakia joined the Eurozone on 1st January 2009, also demonstrating a serious current account imbalance – a deficit of almost 8% of GDP which evidently did not concern the ECB.

It should be reiterated that once countries with serious balance of payments problems have joined the Euro then the possibility of devaluation no longer exists. Thus, having outlined the way that the REER develops, the possibility of reducing these debt inducing deficits is greatly reduced.

Although the Eurozone deficit appears to be modest, too many countries have persistent deficits that would normally be regarded as being 'unsustainable'. The US trade deficit is in the region of 5% to 6% of GDP and has for years been described as being 'unsustainable'. If Germany's trade surplus is subtracted from the aggregated EU figure, then the position of the rest of Europe – with some exceptions – appears to be even more dire. Thus, speculation about Germany herself leaving the Euro has serious implications for the remaining members. As it is, it has been argued that the Euro has served Germany so well that the political class has shown itself, against all its own better instincts, ready to make huge compromises over financial policy in order to preserve the currency.

The Maastricht Criteria include the provision that would-be member-states must have been members of the Exchange Rate Mechanism II for two years and with stable exchange rates. This means that those nations of Eastern Europe and the Baltic States that wish to join are also tied to a strict exchange rate policy. Hitherto, countries such as Hungary and Poland practised a much more pragmatic policy, to offset inflation differentials allowing a staggered devaluation of the Forint and Zloty respectively. To even consider fixing the exchange rates of these countries with their strongest competitors, while running outlandish trade and current account deficits seems inexplicable and potentially very dangerous. As the table below indicates, economic inequalities and the rapid exposure of the domestic markets of these countries to EU imports has created a very dangerous pattern of current account deficits.

Eastern Europe: Current Account Balances

As % GDP	2002	2003	2004	2005	2006	2007	2008	2009
Bulgaria	-2.4	-5.5	-6.6	-12.4	-18.4	-26.9	-24.2	-9.5
Czech Rep.	-5.7	-6.3	-5.3	-1.3	-2.5	-3.3	-0.6	-1.1
Hungary	-7.0	-8.0	-8.4	-7.2	-7.1	-6.5	-7.1	0.2
Poland	-2.8	-2.5	-4.0	-1.2	-2.7	-4.8	-5.1	-1.7
Romania	-3.3	-5.8	-8.4	-9.8	-10.4	-13.4	-11.9	-4.5
Estonia	-10.6	-11.3	-11.3	-10.0	-15.3	-17.0	-9.7	4.5
Latvia	-6.6	-8.1	-12.9	-12.5	-22.5	-22.3	-13.1	8.6
Lithuania	-5.2	-6.9	-7.6	-7.1	-10.7	-14.6	-12.2	4.2
Eastern Europe	-3.1	-4.2	-5,4	-5.1	-6.6	-8.0	-7.9	-2.5

(Source: IMF, *World Economic Outlook*, October 2010)

Of particular interest here are the IMF's ideas about the Baltic States: as can be seen the IMF has been predicting a huge transformation of their current account balances. These countries had achieved spectacular growth rates, fed by incautious lending by the Scandinavian banks – this simply turned these three small economies into market bubbles which collapsed with the onset of the credit crunch. This was all greatly encouraged by the closing interest rate differentials which allowed businesses and citizens to borrow far too cheaply.

Let us be clear about this, the 'convergence play'. The idea was floated that as these and other countries approached Euro membership then their credit status would improve and their risk premium would be reduced. In other words interest payments on government and other debt would fall. This entirely fraudulent notion, encouraged by the powers that be, simply encouraged an orgy of borrowing in countries such as the Baltic States. The market has now restored risk premiums upon the debt of these nations with extremely painful results.

THE BALTIC STATES AND GERMANY: LONG TERM YIELDS

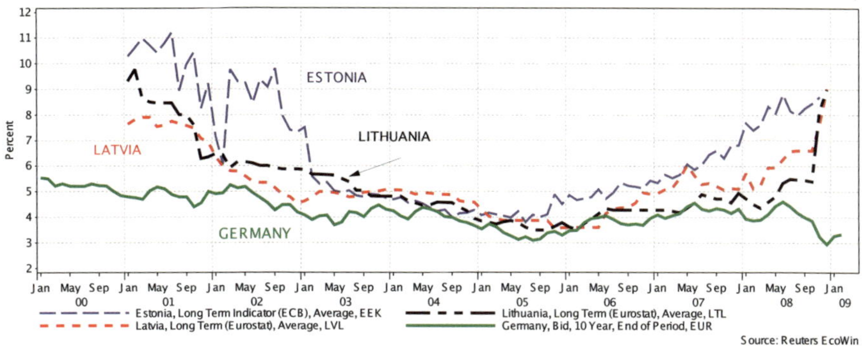

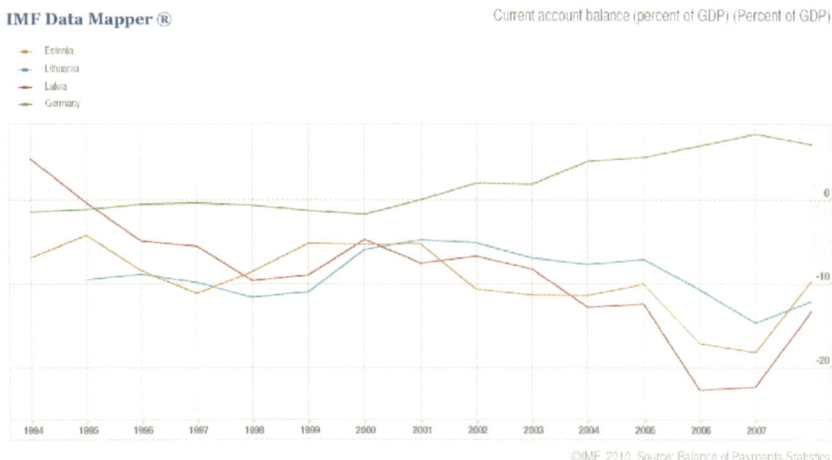

The fragility and deterioration of the financial standing of Eastern Europe is set out in the previous graph and the following table and graph. The first point is that for many years rapid economic growth in Eastern Europe and the Baltics drew in imports and even though export performance has been strong, the trade deficit has tended to widen. This in turn has contributed to the growth of external debt – it does not account for it single-handedly. Rather, the great requirements for capital and for the funding of current consumption has meant that bank lending to the region was very active for a number of years. However, the fact remains that current account deficits, sometimes of serious size, have to be funded and apart from Foreign Direct Investment and official transfers are the only real alternatives to the incurring of government external debt.

Eastern and Central Europe

US $ Bn.	2002	2003	2004	2005	2006	2007	2008	2009
Exports	163.5	210.0	276.2	321.1	386.5	480.7	581.0	449.4
Imports	202.7	264.7	348.9	407.2	498.1	631.3	761.5	524.5
Trade Balance	-39.1	-54.7	-72.7	-86.2	-111.6	-150.7	-180.5	-75.1
Net Services	15.1	19.6	22.8	27.9	27.9	34.4	41.8	39.1
Current Account	-20.1	-33.3	-53.4	-59.8	-87.4	-132.9	-153.0	-40.2
External Debt	327.4	407.2	491.4	536.9	693.5	933.9	1,057.1	1,123.8
Debt Service*	98.8	108.0	139.2	176.9	215.8	267.9	385.6	395.5
Debt/GDP %+	50.7	51.1	49.8	45.7	52.8	56.7	54.5	64.4
As % Exports								
External Debt	154.7	149.9	139.7	131.1	143.0	154.5	144.5	194.5
Debt Service	46.7	39.8	39.7	43.3	44.6	44.5	52.8	68.4
Interest	5.3	4.4	4.0	3.9	4.4	4.6	5.2	5.3
Amortisation	41.4	35.5	35.7	39.4	40.2	39.9	47.6	63.1

*Interest and amortisation payments in US Dollars. +External debt as a % of Gross Domestic Product.

(Source: IMF, *World Economic Outlook*, April 2010, Statistical Appendix)

As is illustrated that debt has grown from $327.3 billion in 2002 to $1,123.8 bn. Last year and the burden of debt service has increased proportionately. To repeat the point, the very idea of these economies 'fixing' their exchange rates against this financial background appears very prejudicial to their own interests and would further detract from what little stability the Euro has left.

The Impossible Dilemma

The political elite of Europe, the architects of the new European order have created an economic and financial disaster that is the Euro and it is evident that they have not the slightest clue as to what to do about its mounting problems. As has been noted, this has come about because of a dangerous mixture of ignorance, self-delusion and Millenarian fervour and sadly, this leaves a number of countries in an impossible quandary. The political class now accepts the notion that some member-states of the Euro would be better off in socio-economic terms if they could leave the Single Currency and restore their monetary autonomy.

This would leave them free to devise their own interest rate policies as befits their economic circumstances. Equally, they could adjust their exchange rate policies so as to avoid the consequences of a severe loss of competitiveness through the workings of the REER.

This is certainly not an argument in favour of competitive devaluations which historically have seldom or ever worked in anything but the very short term, and in most instances not even then. Equally, what we have examined are the destructive consequences of premature monetary union, a union that preceded real economic convergence. The creation of the Euro was precisely this, an error of economic policy that should be corrected before it causes more economic distortions and most importantly of all, before it inflicts further damage upon the economic welfare of European citizens who bear no responsibility for the myopic obsessions of their political masters. As has already been seen in Greece, the loss of economic welfare will inevitably, in accordance with the lessons of history, lead to social and political degeneration.

That is a matter of indifference to the privileged elite who will never suffer deprivation as a result of their own wilful and ill-advised actions – this is what inevitably happens when political actions cannot be questioned by any democratic forum. But what are altogether more serious are the financial consequences of any troubled country leaving the Euro – it is so serious that it is virtually impossible to envisage such a departure unless that country is prepared to default upon its debts.

At the outset of this paper, attention was drawn to the perception of the financial markets that the Euro was facing a growing crisis of confidence and the point is repeated in the two following charts.

10 Year Government Bond Yields – Germany, Italy, Greece, Spain

10 Year Government Bond Yields – Germany, Ireland, Portugal, France

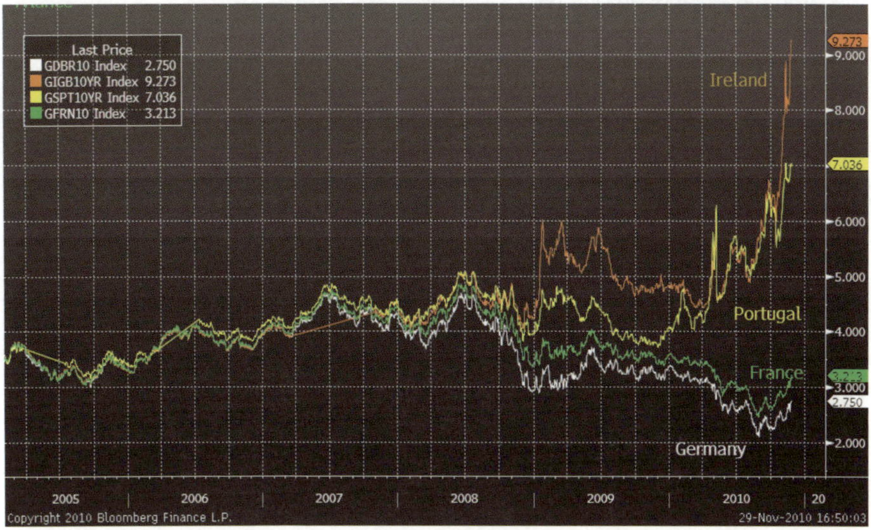

The crux of the problem is that to leave the Euro, with the legacy of large debts denominated in foreign currencies, would be financially ruinous however economically desirable it might be in the long run. The restored currencies would have to be substantially devalued from their 1999 levels in order to restore competitiveness which has been so eroded by the problem of the REER.

But such a devaluation would increase the burden of external debt to a ruinous extent, leaving such countries with the increasingly attractive option of default. It is the case that a large proportion of the external debt in Eastern Europe, as previously illustrated, consists of bank and other loans and credits to the private sector upon which wealth creation and employment ultimately depend.

Defaulting upon government debt is by no means a rare event and is invariably followed by the efforts of agencies such as the International Monetary Fund to negotiate programmes of monetary and fiscal consolidation which would then lead to the financial rehabilitation even of 'serial defaulters'.

This was clearly seen after the Latin Debt crisis of 1981/2 when Brazil, Chile, Mexico and Argentina defaulted. Similarly, the Brady Bond programme initiated in 1989 provided a useful exit strategy for banks and other financial institutions that had foolishly become embroiled in these markets. The Brady programme extended beyond the defaulted Latin American states and included the Philippines, Nigeria, Bulgaria and Poland, among others.

The impact of default, however, is obviously not confined to the government bond markets. The private sector of the economy would suffer grievously from a sharp contraction of liquidity and credit, capital flight, higher taxation, rising unemployment, business failures and social stress – as has been seen in too many instances. Such a sequence of events has been seen too many times in Argentina and elements of it are already evident in Greece and Ireland.

The threat of default is so real that it is recognised at the highest levels of the Brussels establishment and their solution is an attempt at a crude sleight of hand that would not fool the financial markets for one second. Jean Claude Juncker, a former Finance Minister and Prime Minister of Luxembourg, has for long advocated the issuance of European 'government' bonds because in this way Greece (for example) as an issuer of sovereign debt would no longer be so identifiable. Naturally, the German government of Chancellor Merkel is fundamentally opposed to this scheme which is also supported, shamefully, by the 'President' of the European Council, Herman Van Rompuy.

The 'Presidents' advancement of the idea has fallen mostly upon deaf ears: it would reward the fiscally profligate by reducing their borrowing costs thereby encouraging yet more borrowing. It would also penalise the virtuous, most notably Germany, by raising their borrowing costs. Such is the economic and financial Hall of Mirrors that is Brussels. Of course, this clumsy attempt at financial deception would not fool the markets for a second – rather they would recognise it for what it is; a desperate attempt by failed institutions to sustain a failed financial policy. It would bring no comfort to the markets – merely suspicion and doubt.

Very regrettably it is very difficult to envisage any resolution of this problem that is now replete with economic, financial, social and political dangers. The error of policy is so fundamental and so serious that it is virtually impossible to imagine that the perpetrators of this disaster in the making could ever even begin to consider a resolution because any such solution would offend against their ideological prejudices and political vanities.

There is no simple solution to this man-made problem and the ruling elite that brought it about clearly have no idea what to do about the growing crisis of confidence. The situation is made yet more complicated by the fact that the trade and current account imbalances within Europe centre so much upon Germany. This situation could, in theory, be ameliorated if Germany abandoned its mercantilistic policy and gave serious stimulus to domestic demand, thus encouraging imports and deflecting exports back into the domestic economy.

In reality it is much too late in the day for this to achieve a sufficient impact and in any case it is very far from active consideration in Berlin.

When the UK was ejected from the Exchange Rate Mechanism in September 1992, the City celebrated the economic liberation of the country. As the following charts show, both the real and the financial economies benefitted enormously from the correction of a fatally flawed economic policy favoured by John Major, Kenneth Clark and Gordon Brown and many other figures who predicted Britain's downfall if we did not join this absurd arrangement.

THE UK: THE ECONOMY AND INTEREST RATES

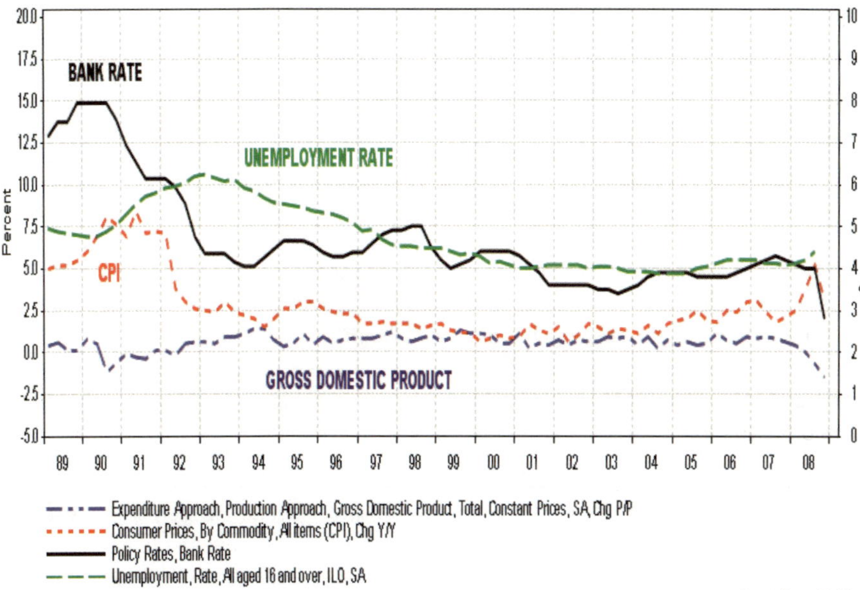

Source: Reuters EcoWin

The liberation from being forced to outbid German interest rates stimulated a period of active economic growth, falling unemployment and moderate inflation. Householders were liberated from murderous mortgage rates, enterprises and output recovered and as the following chart indicates, as Sterling found its appropriate market driven exchange rate, the London Stock Market enjoyed a long bull run. Although the ever mendacious Gordon Brown advocated the revaluation of Sterling with the DMark and higher interest rates, it was he who in 1997 inherited the strongest economy ever bequeathed by an outgoing government to an incoming one.

Unfortunately there can be no such happy ending to the nightmare of the Euro. Although its disintegration would be economically beneficial in the long term, its demise will be extremely destructive in the near to medium term. The example of the UK simply illustrates that there is life after Euro-folly. However, in the same way that we could not expect that the government would deliver Britain from the absurdities of the ERM, so Europe cannot expect that the likes of Herman Van Rompuy, Manuel Barosso, Jean Claude Trichet and the other grandees and potentates of Europe will deliver the Eurozone from the destructive absurdities of the Euro.

UK STERLING AND THE EQUITY MARKET

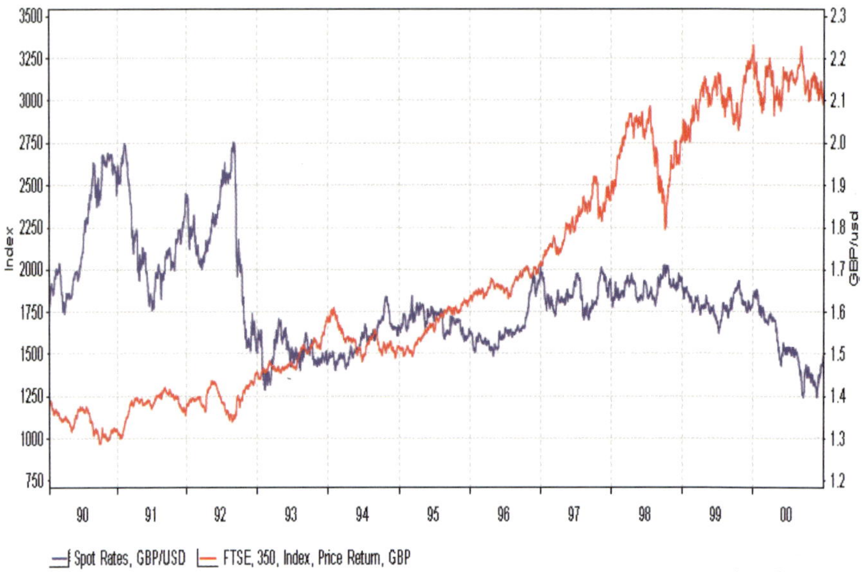

Source: Reuters EcoWin

STATISTICAL APPENDIX
Europe and Beyond – Inflation Rates

	92-01*	2002	2003	2004	2005	2006	2007	2008	2009	2010
Eurozone	2.3	2.3	2.1	2.1	2.2	2.2	2.1	3.3	0.3	1.1
Germany	2.1	1.4	1.0	1.8	1.9	1.8	2.3	2.8	0.1	0.9
France	1.6	1.9	2.2	2.3	1.9	1.9	1.6	3.2	0.1	1.2
Italy	3.3	2.6	2.8	2.3	2.2	2.2	2.0	3.5	0.8	1.4
Spain	3.7	3.6	3.1	3.1	3.4	3.6	2.8	4.1	-0.3	1.2
Netherlands	2.5	3.8	2.2	1.4	1.5	1.7	1.6	2.2	1.0	1.1
Belgium	1.9	1.6	1.5	1.9	2.5	2.3	1.8	4.5	-0.2	1.6
Greece	7.6	3.9	3.4	3.0	3.5	3.3	3.0	4.2	1.4	1.9
Austria	1.9	1.7	1.3	2.0	2.1	1.7	2.2	3.2	0.4	1.3
Portugal	4.0	3.7	3.3	2.5	2.1	3.0	2.4	2.7	-0.9	0.8
Finland	1.8	2.0	1.3	0.1	0.8	1.3	1.6	3.9	1.6	1.1
Ireland	2.7	4.7	4.0	2.3	2.2	2.7	2.9	3.1	-1.7	-2.0
Slovakia	-	3.5	8.4	7.5	2.8	4.3	1.9	3.9	0.9	0.8
Slovenia	-	7.5	5.6	3.6	2.5	2.5	3.6	5.7	0.8	1.5
Luxembourg	2.1	2.1	2.0	2.2	2.5	2.7	2.3	3.4	0.8	1.0
Cyprus	3.1	2.6	1.9	2.7	2.5	2.6	0.7	4.7	1.8	2.0
Malta	3.1	2.6	1.9	2.7	2.5	2.6	0.7	4.7	1.8	2.0
Advanced**	2.4	1.6	1.8	2.0	2.3	2.4	2.2	3.4	0.1	1.5
USA	2.7	1.6	2.3	2.7	3.4	3.2	2.9	3.8	-0.3	2.1
UK	2.1	1.3	1.4	1.3	2.0	2.3	2.3	3.6	2.2	2.7

*Annual average. ** Advanced economies as defined by the IMF.
(Source: IMF, *World Economic Outlook*, April 2010)

NOTES

NOTES

NOTES

NOTES

NOTES

One letter from Baroness Ludford
and others (Turkish Cypriot Plight,
June 30)

THE BRUGES GROUP | ASSOCIATE MEMBERSHIP

TEL: +44 (0)20 7287 4414 | www.brugesgroup.com/join | info@brugesgroup.com

To join the Bruges Group, complete the following form and send it to the Membership Secretary with your annual subscription fee. This will entitle you to receive our published material for one year. It also helps cover the cost of the numerous Bruges Group meetings to which all Associate Members are invited. **You can also join online, right now, by using your debit or credit card. Please log on to www.brugesgroup.com/join or you can join over the phone by calling 020 7287 4414.**

Minimum Associate Membership Rates for 1 year UK Member £30 ☐ , Europe £45 ☐ , Rest of the world £60 ☐

Optional donation: £10 ☐ £20 ☐ £50 ☐ £100 ☐ £250 ☐ £500 ☐

Other, please specify: ....

If you are able to give more towards our work, we would be very grateful for your support. For the sake of convenience, we urge you to pay by standing order.

YES ! I wish to join the Bruges Group

Title: .... Name: ....

Address: ....

.... Postcode: ....

Telephone: ....

Email: ....

BANKERS ORDER Name and full postal address of your Bank or Building Society

To: The Manager:.................................... Bank/Building Society

Address: ....

.... Postcode: ....

Account number: .... Sort code: ....

Please Pay: Barclays Bank Ltd (Sort Code 20-46-73), 6 Clarence St, Kingston-upon-Thames, Surrey KT1 1NY

The sum of £ .... (figures)

Signature: .... Date: ....

to the credit of the Bruges Group A/C No 90211214 forthwith and on the same day in each subsequent year until further notice.

— or —

CHEQUE PAYMENTS I enclose a cheque made payable to the Bruges Group

The sum of £ .... (figures)

Signature: .... Date: ....

— or —

MEMBERSHIP PAYMENT BY CREDIT/DEBIT CARD

Solo ☐ Visa Card ☐ Visa Delta ☐ Visa Electron ☐ Mastercard ☐ JCB ☐ Switch ☐

Card number: ....

Valid from: .... Expiry date: ....Issue number: .... Security code: ....

Card holder's name as it appears on the card (please print): ....

.Address of card holder: ....

.... Postcode: ....

Telephone:..

Email: .... Signature: .... Date: ....

The Bruges Group

www.brugesgroup.com

Please complete this form and return to:
The Membership Secretary, The Bruges Group, 227 Linen Hall, 162-168 Regent St., London W1B 5TB